LOVE BETTER

A Sacred Journey Back to You

Anzé Mofor

Reclaim Your Heart • Rewire Your Patterns •
Rewrite Your Love Story

Published by Project ICON

Digital ISBN: 978-1-969888-25-0
Paperback ISBN: 978-1-969888-27-4
Hardback ISBN: 978-1-969888-26-7

https://projecticon.io/

Acknowledgements

To the One Who Was the Wind Beneath My Wings

Kakwa Emmanuel Yuh

Thank you for being the quiet strength beneath me when I was still learning how to fly.

You supported me in ways that went far beyond what anyone could see: personally, financially, mentally, emotionally. You gave me something rare and sacred: space. Space to stumble. Space to question. Space to mess up without being diminished. Space to choose me and grow without being rushed.

When I didn't yet trust myself, you trusted me. When I doubted my footing, you held the ground steady beneath me. You never tried to control my becoming, only to protect it.

Because of you, I learned that support doesn't suffocate; it liberates.

And for that, I will always be grateful.

With love and deep appreciation,
Anzé

To the Ones Who Held Me Down When My Mind Ran Wild

Fotema Mba, Melaine Ndi Pegebe, and Evelyn Frazer Ndi

Thank you for being my mirror, my anchor, and my sounding board when my ideas came faster than my certainty.

You gave me something invaluable: honest love. Not flattery. Not ego-stroking. But truth wrapped in care. You challenged me gently, questioned me lovingly, and reminded me of my values when I momentarily lost sight of them.

When I doubted my own thoughts, you helped me untangle them.

When I questioned my direction, you reminded me of my compass.

When I felt unsteady, you held me down: not to limit me, but to stabilize me.

Your presence taught me that real support doesn't silence brilliance, it grounds it.

Thank you for holding me steady when I needed it most.

Love you now and Always,
Anzé

To the Woman Who Introduced Me to My Femininity

Rori Raye

There was a world inside me that I didn't know had a name until you showed me.

You introduced me to femininity: not as weakness, but as power. Not as performance, but as presence. Not as something to earn, but something to embody.

Through your gentle, steady coaching, I learned to see myself as a siren, a goddess, a woman deeply connected to her essence. You didn't rush me. You didn't harden me. You didn't ask me to become someone else.

You helped me remember who I already was.

Because of you, I softened without shrinking. I opened without losing discernment. I claimed my queenhood without apology.

Thank you for awakening a language within me that now guides how I love, live, and lead.

With deep gratitude,
Anzé

To the Father Figure I Didn't Know I Needed

Mr. Stedman Graham

Some words change a life not because they are loud, but because they arrive at the right moment.

When you said to me, "Focus on yourself. The rest is an illusion," something shifted permanently inside me. In that sentence, I saw myself clearly. I recognized how, for a time, I had stepped away from my own center while chasing what only appeared meaningful on the outside, attempting to solidify my identity within illusions rather than truth.

You didn't lecture. You didn't overexplain. You simply spoke the truth and trusted it to land.

That glimpse of grounded leadership, clarity, and calm authority, gave me permission to reclaim my focus, my energy, and my greatness. Learning first to lead myself so I may better lead and influence others.

Thank you for reminding me that leadership often sounds like a few words spoken well, and for being a living example to young leaders around the world.

With deep reverence,
Anzé

To My Dear Friend and Gentle Guide

Jonathan Marshal White

Thank you for meeting me from a man's perspective with softness, patience, and presence.

Through your gentle coaching, you helped me drop my shoulders, quiet the inner tension, and take intentional action toward the peace I was seeking, not externally, but within myself.

You reminded me that strength does not require force, and clarity does not require urgency. And somehow, in your calm, I found my own.

Your hugs are healing because they are grounded.

Your guidance is powerful because it is clean.

Your friendship is rare because it is safe.

Thank you for being exactly who you are, and for offering that presence so generously.

With love and appreciation,
Anzé

To the Couple Who Showed Me Love Is Real

Miriam and Daniel Dvorsky

I once believed a love like yours was an illusion, beautiful, perhaps, but unrealistic.

And then I met you.

Through your kindness, your gentleness, and your perfectly imperfect partnership, you showed me love as something lived, not performed. Observing you taught me that love does not need perfection to be profound; it needs presence, compassion, and choice.

Even in the face of loss, losing your home to the Palisades fire, you opened your hearts, your space, and your lives to me. That generosity shifted something deep within my spirit.

Your love raised my frequency. Your resilience expanded my capacity. Your example rewired what I believed was possible.

Thank you for being living proof that love, abundance, and fulfillment can coexist, even in adversity.

With a grateful heart,
Anzé

Foreword

By Rori Raye

There comes a moment in a woman's life when achievement is no longer the answer.

Not because success is wrong, far from it, but because success alone cannot hold her. It cannot soothe her nervous system, soften her heart, or restore her center. It cannot receive her.

Many women who will find themselves in these pages are accomplished, capable, intelligent, and strong. They have learned how to lead, build, survive, and succeed. They have learned how to carry responsibility and often, how to carry far too much of it alone.

What they may have forgotten is something far more subtle and far more powerful.

How to *be* a woman in a modern world.

Not in the way culture defines femininity. Not in performance. Not in compliance. But in essence.

To be a woman is to have a center that can soften without collapsing. To lean back without disengaging. To receive without apology. To allow life, love, and even clarity to come *to* her rather than always reaching outward.

This book is not asking you to give up your strength. It is inviting you to **release the tension that strength can quietly create** when it is never allowed to rest.

Leaning back does not mean doing less. It means **returning to yourself**, to open up and welcome what nurtures your soul.

It is a reset of the nervous system. Remembering your body. A steadying of your inner world.

From this place, discernment sharpens. Boundaries become cleaner. Desire becomes clearer. And love, starting with the love you extend to yourself, can finally move freely.

What Anzé offers here is not instruction, but invitation. Not force, but permission. Permission to soften. Permission to pause. Permission to receive. Permission to just be, with the sweetness of nothing.

Not for a man. Not for approval. But for your own alignment. When a woman is truly centered, she does not disappear; she **emerges**. And from that emergence, everything else finds its natural order: love, leadership, connection, and fulfillment begin to flow with ease rather than force.

This is when she opens like a lotus rooted in stillness, rising through depth, unfolding with grace. Beautiful and strong, she does not demand attention, yet she transforms the space around her, offering beauty, wisdom, and a quiet, undeniable power.

With warmth and trust in your becoming,
Rori Raye

INTRODUCTION

"I used to believe love meant being chosen to prove I was worthy and enough."

For years, that belief lived in my bones like a second pulse. I performed, pleased, and prayed my way into rooms where my truth felt too loud, where the fullness of who I was seemed like too much to offer and not enough to keep. I learned early how to shrink. How to soften my voice when it wanted to roar. How to smile through confusion and call it grace. I thought that was love. I thought that was what it meant to be a woman worth staying for.

Childhood conditioning quietly wrote my standards long before I knew I had the pen. The lessons came disguised as protection, wrapped in the voices of people who meant well but were also wounded. Western love myths choreographed my expectations with precision, teaching me to wait, to hope, to measure my value by who reached for me. Disney promised rescue. Romantic comedies promised transformation through a man's gaze. Social media sold a checklist of tall, successful, and picture-perfect, as if love were something you could order from a catalog. Neither taught me how to be at home in my own heart. Neither prepared me for the silence that comes when you realize you have been building your life in someone else's house.

This book is not a "how to get a partner" manual. There are enough of those already, and most of them will leave you more lost than when you started. This is something different. This is a come-home guide. A bridge from survival love to soulful love. Breaking its survival contract. From being chosen by others to choosing yourself first, fiercely and without apology and understanding yourself, your identity and your soul. Within these pages, you will laugh at the absurdity of what we once accepted. You will cry as old wounds finally find words. And most of all, you will remember who you are beneath the roles, the performances, and the years of forgetting.

Each chapter ends with reflection, affirmation, and a small act of courage, because healing is not passive. It asks something of us. We are not here to chase fantasies or to rehearse the same painful patterns with new faces. We are here to build truth. To construct something real from the ruins of what we thought love was supposed to be.

Welcome to the journey back to yourself. She has been waiting.

Table of Contents

Foreword 9

INTRODUCTION 12

CHAPTER ONE: When Love Hurts but You Can't Let Go 17

CHAPTER TWO: The Roles We Wear to Be Loved 45

CHAPTER THREE: Why We Repeat What Broke Us 64

CHAPTER FOUR: I Am the Love I've Been Waiting For 83

CHAPTER FIVE: The Love That Was Good but Not Enough 103

CHAPTER SIX: The Power of Emotional Safety... 115

CHAPTER SEVEN: Self-Trust and the Woman Within..134

CHAPTER EIGHT: Soulful Love Deserves a Soulful You..152

CHAPTER NINE: When the World Forgets What Love Looks Like..170

CHAPTER TEN: From Survival to Soulmate....189

CHAPTER ELEVEN: Love Is the Oxygen: A Return to the Heart..210

EPILOGUE: Why We Love. Why We Exist......229

A Letter to My Future Children..........................236

CHAPTER ONE

When Love Hurts but You Can't Let Go

"Some wounds don't bleed. They bond."

I stayed in a relationship that looked perfect on paper and felt empty in my body. From the outside, we made sense. We checked boxes. We smiled for pictures. But inside, where truth lives and the soul keeps its own accounting, something was slowly dying. I could feel it in the mornings when I woke up next to someone and still felt alone. I could feel it in the way I started measuring my words before I spoke them, editing myself in real time, shrinking my presence to fit into spaces that were never designed to hold all of me.

My voice got quieter. Not all at once, but gradually, the way a flame reduces itself when the oxygen is slowly pulled from the room. My light dimmed. My laughter became careful, calculated, stripped of its spontaneity. I told myself I was being loyal, that this was what commitment looked like, that real love required sacrifice and the willingness to endure. But underneath that noble story was a truth I could not yet face: I was afraid. Afraid to start over. Afraid to face the mirror and see a woman who had traded her wholeness for the illusion of being chosen. Afraid to admit I was building a future out of what my abnormal and painful past had normalized, that if I stopped earning love, it would leave, and I might never find it again.

I felt like I was tolerated. Not celebrated. Not cherished. Just tolerated. And I accepted it because somewhere along the way, I had convinced myself that tolerance was the best I could get. That wanting more was greedy. That asking for depth and presence and genuine affection was asking too much from a world that had already given me so little. With my religious conditioning, it felt noble. Though I knew it was not honest. I was raised to take what I could get and not complain even if I was dying inside.

It wasn't the first time I mistook pain for passion, or endurance for love. I had a long history of confusing intensity with intimacy, of believing that the harder something was to hold on to, the more valuable it must be. And yet, every time I ignored that ache in my chest, every time I pushed down the knowing that rose up from my gut, I was subconsciously whispering to my nervous system: "Hush. We'll deal with it later. Right now, we need to keep this together, because people are watching.". Little did I know, I was resubscribing to a survival contract I could not sustain.

Later came. And it came like a storm that had been gathering on the horizon for years, patient and inevitable, waiting for the moment when I could no longer outrun it. I was an avalanche on the inside, still trying to keep up appearances on the outside.

The Devastation of Decline

Love that hurts often begins as love that "almost" fits. That is the cruelest part. It is not obviously wrong. It is not dramatically toxic in the ways that would make leaving easy. It is just slightly off, like a shoe that is a half size too small. You can still walk in it. You can even convince yourself it fits. But over time, it will bruise you in places no one else can see.

Intensity masquerades as intimacy. You mistake the rush of adrenaline for the warmth of connection. The highs feel so high that you become willing to endure the lows, not realizing that real love is not supposed to feel like a rollercoaster you cannot get off of. Chemistry drowns out character. You are so intoxicated by the pull, by the magnetic force of attraction, that you ignore the red flags waving in your peripheral vision. You tell yourself that love will change them, that your devotion will be enough, that time will smooth out the rough edges.

And slowly, so slowly you almost do not notice, you become agreeable, then invisible. You stop voicing your opinions. You stop advocating for your needs. You become a supporting character in your own love story, always adjusting, always accommodating, always making yourself smaller so there is more room for someone else. You are tolerated, not treasured. And the difference between those two things is the difference between surviving and thriving.

It is not that you do not know better. It is that you have been conditioned, by childhood, by culture, by a thousand small messages absorbed before you were old enough to question them. You learned to see struggle as proof of loyalty, chaos as chemistry, and overgiving as the purest form of love. If someone gave me any attention, it validated my sense of worth, even though deep down inside, in the quiet spaces where truth refuses to be silenced, I was screaming for help. I was drowning in plain sight, and I had convinced myself that the drowning was devotion.

"But God never asked you to bleed to be blessed."

The Breaking That Began the Becoming

Like Dr. Joe Dispenza wrote, "No human can survive in emergency mode for a long period of time." I was living proof of that truth. My body had become a battlefield, and I was losing the war I did not even know I was fighting. Every time I silenced my truth to keep the peace, every time I shrank to stay lovable, every time I betrayed my own knowing to preserve a relationship that was slowly consuming me, my body kept score. It was recording everything I refused to say, storing every swallowed word, every suppressed sob, every moment of self-abandonment in its tissues and cells.

At first, it was small things. Headaches that came without explanation. Bloating that no dietary change could resolve. Weight gain that seemed disconnected from what I ate. Fatigue that sleep could not touch. I explained it away, the way we do when we are not ready to face what our bodies are trying to tell us. Then came the insomnia, the nights spent staring at the ceiling while my mind raced through every conversation, every perceived failure, every way I might have done better. Panic attacks that arrived without warning, my heart pounding so hard I thought it might escape my chest. Digestive issues that made eating feel like a negotiation. And finally, anemia, my body literally unable to produce enough blood to sustain the life I was living.

I told myself it was fatigue from work. I told myself it was stress. I told myself it was aging, that this was simply what happened to women in their thirties who were trying to hold too many things together. But the truth? My body was not betraying me. It was protecting me from my own neglect. It was sending me messages I refused to read, alarms I kept hitting snooze on, warnings I dismissed as weakness.

As Carolyn Myss reminds us in *Anatomy of the Spirit*, "Illness is a physical manifestation of spiritual and emotional energy gone awry." My spirit had been whispering for years, "Slow down. Pay attention. You are losing yourself." But I was too busy being strong. Too addicted to proving I could handle anything. Too committed to the performance of having it all together. Until life's tragedies and grief got me in a chokehold, and I was forced to accept what I had been running from: I could not do this anymore. Not like this.

I found myself in a hospital bed at UCLA, pale and terrified, my hemoglobin dangerously low. The fluorescent lights above me buzzed with an indifferent hum, casting everything in a harsh, clinical glow that made my skin look like paper. I needed a blood transfusion. My emotional numbness had given me the facade that things were not that bad, that I could keep pushing through, that my body would eventually catch up with my will. But then I started having blackouts. Moments where the world would simply disappear, leaving me disoriented and frightened in places I did not remember walking to.

I had driven myself to the ER that night. I remember the surreal quality of the drive, the way the streetlights seemed to blur and stretch, the way my hands gripped the steering wheel with a desperation that had nothing to do with traffic. The next thing I knew, I was surrounded by seven people, their faces a blur of concern and professional focus. I was alone. Scared. Afraid that this might be the end of everything.

They told me my blood count was so low it was not normal for me to have been driving. That I should not have been conscious, let alone operating a vehicle. Some of them were teaching doctors; some were students. Their youth did not comfort me. If anything, it made me feel like a specimen, a case study, a problem to be solved. I remember thinking, in my fear-addled state, that I was about to become a guinea pig for people who had never seen someone like me before.

Inside, beneath the beeping monitors and the cold hospital sheets, I prayed. Not the polished prayers of Sunday mornings, but the raw, desperate pleading of someone who has finally hit the bottom they did not believe existed.

"God, if I do not go now, I promise I will love and care for myself better. I will not neglect me again. I will not abandon myself for anyone. I will learn to treat my body as sacred ground, not a sacrifice to lay on the altar of someone else's comfort."

That was a rebirth. Not the dramatic kind you see in movies, with swelling music and immediate transformation. But the quiet, profound kind that happens in hospital beds and dark nights of the soul, when you finally stop dying for love and start living for truth.

Recovery was not a single moment. It was years of relearning how to live intentionally, gently, honestly. It was a daily practice of choosing myself, even when that choice felt selfish, even when the old voices told me I was being too much, asking too much, expecting too much. I changed my diet, learning to nourish my body instead of punishing it. I changed my schedule, creating space for rest instead of filling every moment with productivity. I changed my circle, letting go of relationships that required me to shrink in order to belong.

I no longer surrounded myself with people who confused my boundaries for attitude, who interpreted my self-respect as arrogance, who could not handle a woman who was learning to take up space unapologetically. I became protective of my peace and conscious of the energy I brought into a room, understanding finally that I was not responsible for managing everyone else's emotions at the expense of my own.

Slowly, I started feeling a version of me I had lost. The girl who once laughed freely, without wondering if her joy was too loud or her happiness too visible. The woman who once dreamed wildly, without immediately dismissing her desires as unrealistic or undeserved. The spirit that once trusted easily, before betrayal taught her that opening her heart was a risk not worth taking.

She was still there. She had been there all along, buried under layers of duty, heartbreak, and unrealistic expectations. Waiting. Patient. Ready to emerge whenever I was ready to welcome her home.

The Cost of Outsourcing Your Peace

When you place your peace in someone else's hands, you will always be negotiating. You will wake up each morning wondering what mood they will be in, calculating how to navigate their emotions, strategizing how to keep the harmony that your well-being depends on. You will bend your boundaries to keep the "good moments" coming, and you will call it love. You will sacrifice your needs to avoid conflict, and you will call it maturity. You will silence your truth to maintain connection, and you will call it compromise.

It is not love. It is emotional debt. It is a transaction where you keep paying and paying, hoping that eventually the balance will be settled, that eventually your investment will yield the return you have been promised. But the return never comes, because you are playing a game where the rules keep changing, where the goalposts keep moving, where enough is never actually enough.

A Pivot of Attention

Lasting intimacy begins when you bring the attention home. Away from what he did or did not do. Away from analyzing his behavior, decoding his texts, interpreting his silences. Into the quiet room of your own heart, where the real work has always been waiting.

Even when he is wrong, the work of liberation is yours. Not because his behavior is acceptable, not because you should tolerate mistreatment, but because your healing cannot be held hostage to someone else's growth. You must ask yourself: What is this stirring up in me? What pattern am I protecting? What part of me still thinks pain is proof of love? What wound is being activated that existed long before he ever arrived?

This is not about letting him off the hook. This is about taking yourself off the hook of waiting for him to change before you can be free.

The Cost of Self-Abandonment

After I left that hospital, I started noticing the trail of quiet betrayals I had normalized. The accumulated evidence of a life lived in service to everyone but myself. I had been so focused on being good, on being acceptable, on being worthy of love, that I had systematically abandoned every part of me that did not fit the mold I thought I needed to fill.

I noticed how often I said "yes" when my body screamed "no." How I would override my own instincts, dismiss my own discomfort, push past my own limits because saying no felt selfish, felt difficult, felt dangerous. I noticed how I laughed off disrespect to keep the peace, turning insults into jokes, minimizing mistreatment so I would not have to confront it, so I would not have to make anyone uncomfortable with my pain.

I noticed how I performed perfection while privately unraveling, presenting a polished exterior while my interior was chaos, smiling through gatherings while crying in my car afterward, pretending to have it all together while silently falling apart.

Each act of self-abandonment is a spiritual paper cut. Small. Almost imperceptible. Easy to dismiss. But eventually, those paper cuts bled into illness, anxiety, and disconnection from the very self I was supposed to be protecting. I had accepted apologies that arrived without repair, giving people credit for words while ignoring the absence of change. I had received just enough hope to keep me investing and just enough confusion to keep me doubting my own worth, my own perception, my own right to ask for more.

The truth is that love cannot heal what dishonesty protects. You cannot build something real on a foundation of performance and pretense. The cracks will always show. The structure will always eventually fail.

When the Body Becomes the Messenger

Our emotions do not vanish when ignored. They do not dissolve simply because we refuse to acknowledge them. They reroute. They find alternative pathways. They store themselves in the body, in muscles and organs and tissues, accumulating interest until the body can no longer hold them. Until something has to give.

The gut tightens where truth is swallowed. All those words you could not say, all those boundaries you could not enforce, all those moments when you knew something was wrong but talked yourself out of knowing. The throat closes where words go unspoken. The voice you silenced to keep the peace now refuses to work at all, closing up when you need it most, trapping everything inside. The heart aches where boundaries have been crossed too many times. Not metaphorically, but literally, carrying the weight of every violation, every dismissal, every time someone walked over a line you had drawn, and you pretended not to notice.

I used to pray for God to take the pain away. To lift it from me like a burden I could not carry, to make it disappear so I could go back to functioning, to performing, to pretending. Now I understand something different. He was not trying to take the pain away. He was trying to teach me to listen to it. To honor it as the messenger it was. To understand that my body was not my enemy but my ally, desperately trying to get my attention, to wake me up, to save me from a life that was slowly killing me.

Because as long as you are performing to be loved, you are teaching your body that safety is conditional. That rest must be earned. That you are only worthy of care when you are producing, achieving, pleasing, proving. And a body that believes safety is conditional can never truly rest. It remains vigilant, on guard, waiting for the next threat, the next test, the next moment when love might be withdrawn.

Reconnecting with the Little Girl Within

When I began my healing journey in earnest, I found her again. The little girl I had buried under accomplishments, heartbreak, and ambition. The child who had learned too early that love was something you earned, not something you received simply for existing. The small one who had watched the adults around her and concluded that her needs were too much, her feelings too big, her very presence a burden to be minimized.

She was not angry, this little girl. That surprised me. I expected her to be furious at all the ways I had neglected her, all the times I had pushed past her protests, all the moments I had chosen someone else's comfort over her safety. But she was not angry. She was just waiting. Waiting for clarity. Waiting to be seen. Waiting to be heard. Waiting to be nurtured in the way she had always deserved and never received.

I began re-parenting her. It felt strange at first, this practice of talking to a part of myself as if she were separate, as if she needed tending. But she did. She needed everything I had failed to give her. I spoke softly to her, the way I wished someone had spoken to me when I was small. I let her cry without trying to fix it or rush her through it. I let her rest without demanding productivity as payment. I let her sit with feelings, teaching her that emotions were not emergencies to be managed but experiences to be felt and moved through.

Slowly, she began to trust me again. Slowly, she stopped bracing for abandonment. Slowly, she started to believe that I would not leave her the way others had, that I would not sacrifice her on the altar of someone else's approval.

Together, we began building new memories. Ones filled with truth instead of performance. Ease instead of constant striving. Laughter that did not have to be earned. Grace that was given freely, not as a reward for good behavior.

And that is when I realized: The woman I was becoming was not new. She was who I had always been before the world told me who I was not, before conditioning taught me to perform for what I inherently deserved. She was original. She was authentic. She had been waiting for me to come home to her all along.

If I could reimagine pain from the past, I could also reimagine the future. This was a revelation that changed everything. Because the mind time-travels constantly, replaying old hurts like movies on an endless loop, rehearsing future fears as if worry could somehow protect us from disappointment. But if the mind could travel to painful places, it could also travel to healing ones.

Just as I could revisit a painful memory and feel the sting as fresh as the day it happened, I could rewrite it with compassion. I could go back in thought, hold that version of me who was hurting, and whisper: "You are safe now. You can rest. What happened was not your fault. You did the best you could with what you knew. And I am here now to give you everything you needed then."

It is not about pretending the pain never happened. It is not about toxic positivity or spiritual bypassing. It is about refusing to let old pain become your life's blueprint. About choosing to build from the present moment rather than from the ruins of the past.

Like Oprah said in her book *What Happened to You?*, "People are not broken. They're doing their best with what happened to them." This shifted everything for me. I was not broken. I had never been broken. I was a whole person responding to circumstances that were often beyond my control, adapting as best I could, surviving in ways that served me then even if they no longer served me now.

A Biblical Parallel

Scripture tells us: "Come to me, all you who are weary and burdened, and I will give you rest." (Matthew 11:28)

God never intended love to feel like constant exhaustion. He never designed intimacy to drain you of everything you have. He intended love to be a refuge, not a race. A shelter, not a storm. A place where you could lay down your armor, not a battlefield where you had to keep it on to survive.

But to rest in love, you must first rest in truth. You must be honest about what you have been accepting. You must be willing to see clearly what has cost you your peace. Sometimes, God will allow what you idolize to break your heart, not because He is cruel, but because He wants you to finally worship the Healer instead of the hurt, to cherish the healing instead of clinging to the wound.

Reflection

What version of "love" did I learn as a child? What did the adults around me model? What did I conclude about what love required of me?

What does my body say when my mouth says, "It's fine"? What sensations arise? What tightens, aches, or shuts down?

Where have I confused struggle with devotion? Where have I believed that pain was proof of depth?

What would rest look like if I stopped earning love? What would I do differently if I believed I was already worthy?

Affirmation

I no longer confuse love with struggle. I listen to my body, honor my truth, and let peace lead me home. I am worthy of love that does not cost me myself.

Closing Truth

You cannot love deeply if you live dishonestly. You cannot build intimacy on self-abandonment. And you cannot meet anyone soul-to-soul while living split in two, performing one thing while feeling another, saying yes while meaning no, smiling while breaking.

When love hurts but you cannot let go, pause. Breathe. Look honestly at what you are holding on to and what it is costing you. It might not be the relationship you need to end. It might be the performance. It might be the version of yourself you created to be acceptable. It might be the belief that you must earn what should be given freely.

Because the day you stop betraying yourself for love is the day love becomes safe enough to stay. The day you stop abandoning yourself for connection is the day connection becomes real. The day you choose your truth over someone else's comfort is the day you finally come home.

And home is where healing begins.

THE YEAR EVERYTHING CHANGED

And So Did I

2020 hit all of us like a plot twist none of us auditioned for. The world we knew, the plans we made, the futures we assumed were guaranteed—all of it dissolved in a matter of weeks. We were given the same world, the same twenty-four hours, the same fear that crept into our homes through news broadcasts and worried phone calls from loved ones. The same masks covering our faces. The same "breaking news" alerts that felt, at times, like fiction written by someone with a particularly dark imagination.

And right in the middle of all that collective chaos, I was sitting with my own personal apocalypse. A furlough notice in one hand, hospital paperwork in the other. I was recovering from surgery, helping my father fight cancer, and praying I would not lose my apartment. The ground beneath me had given way, and I was in freefall with no parachute in sight.

But in the strangest way, that year gave me something unexpected. It forced the whole world to sit still. And in that collective stillness, for the first time in years, I finally heard myself. Not the version of me that performed for approval. Not the version that stayed busy to avoid feeling. But the real me, the one who had been whispering beneath all the noise, waiting for me to get quiet enough to listen.

The Gift Hidden in Crisis

Lockdown gave me two things I did not realize I needed: silence and a mirror. The silence came first, uncomfortable and unrelenting. Without the distraction of commuting, socializing, and staying perpetually busy, I was left alone with my thoughts. And my thoughts, it turned out, had a lot to say.

I finally had time to ask myself questions I had been avoiding for years. Questions that had been lurking at the edges of my consciousness, waiting for a moment when I could no longer outrun them.

"What do I really want?" Not what I was told to want. Not what looked impressive. Not what would make others comfortable. What did I at my core actually desire for my life?

"Why do I not believe I deserve the life I secretly dream about?" Why did my biggest dreams feel like fantasies reserved for other people, while I settled for a smaller existence that felt "realistic"?

"Why am I always taking care of everyone but me?" Why did self-sacrifice feel like virtue while self-care felt like selfishness? Where had I learned this backwards equation?

It reminded me of the scripture: "Love your neighbor as yourself." (Mark 12:31) We quote it constantly, but what no one tells you is this: You cannot love your neighbor if you do not love yourself first. The love you extend to others can only be as deep as the love you have cultivated within. You cannot pour from an empty vessel. You cannot give what you have never received, including from yourself.

Self-love is not vanity. It is not narcissism or selfishness dressed up in spiritual language. It is responsibility. It is survival. It is obedience to a God who created you with intention and does not want to see His creation neglected, not even by you.

Just like the airplane safety rule tells us: "Put your oxygen mask on first before helping others." In 2020, my oxygen mask was hanging low, dangling just out of reach, and I was out here trying to assist the entire cabin. I was saving everyone while suffocating myself. And that year, that terrible beautiful year, forced me to finally grab my own mask and breathe.

The Failed Business, the Faith, and the Fantasy Life

I started an online business during that time. I poured what little energy and resources I had into something that felt like hope. And I failed. Not a little. Completely. The kind of failure that leaves you staring at your bank account wondering how you are going to eat next week.

I tried again. Failed harder. Lost money I did not even have, digging myself into a hole while trying to climb out of one. I can only imagine what my conversations with God sounded like from His perspective. Here I was, making the same mistakes, expecting different results, insisting I knew better while clearly knowing nothing at all.

But something in me refused to quit. Not because I was confident. I was terrified. Not because I had a clear plan. I was making it up as I went. But because survival has a way of pushing you into courage you did not know you possessed. When your back is against the wall and the only options are give up or keep moving, something primal kicks in. Something that refuses to let the story end this way.

Then one day, after crying on a friend's couch, mascara streaking my face, feeling like the biggest failure who had ever attempted anything, I sat down and wrote something I had not written in years: a vision.

Not a to-do list. Not a budget with desperate numbers and impossible timelines. A vision. A picture of the life I wanted to live, detailed and specific and completely detached from my current reality.

I closed my eyes and let myself feel it. Really feel it, not just think about it. A week on an island somewhere tropical, warm sand beneath my feet and no deadlines waiting. Two dress sizes down, not for anyone else but for the way I wanted to feel in my own body. A sports car that I had always wanted but never believed I deserved. A home that felt like a vacation, a sanctuary instead of just a place to sleep. Eating fruits I had never tasted from countries I had never visited. Snorkeling for the first time, my body suspended in clear blue water, surrounded by life. Launching my youth nonprofit in Beverly Hills. Caring for my dad with time and presence and dignity, not rushed visits squeezed between obligations. A relationship with a man who was kind, aligned, emotionally mature, athletic, stylish, and soft with me. A family of my own someday.

I laughed at myself when I finished writing. It felt ridiculous. Delusional, even. Here I was, barely able to pay rent, mapping out a life that belonged in a magazine. But the moment I saw it in my mind, something shifted. It felt more real than my current circumstances. Truer than the struggle I was living. As if this vision was the reality and my present situation was the temporary illusion.

I did not have the money to make any of it happen. But I took a small loan and tried the business again. This time, with intention. This time, with humility. This time, with a foundation of self-love that had been missing from every previous attempt.

The Manifestation Unfolded

And God showed off. There is no other way to describe it. He took my trembling faith and my imperfect efforts, and He multiplied them in ways I still struggle to articulate.

In 2021, I moved into a home I had visualized, palm trees and all, exactly as I had seen it in my mind's eye. I bought the Maserati, the car I had always wanted and never believed I would own. I traveled to Tahiti and Fiji, spending a week on each island, swimming in waters so clear they looked artificial, eating fruits whose names I had to look up, living the exact life I had written down on that tear-stained paper.

In 2022, I met a man I still call "perfectly imperfect." He checked boxes I did not even know I had, qualities I had not thought of asking for because I did not know they existed. We loved each other. We learned from each other. We grew together. And when it ended, we honored each other with grace, refusing to turn our story into a tragedy just because it did not last forever.

That same year, I launched my nonprofit at the Beverly Hills Hotel, a venue where I had once worked in a completely different capacity, now returning as the founder, the visionary, the woman who had turned her pain into purpose. I did it in honor of my mentor and my other mother, the women who had believed in me when I could not believe in myself.

In 2023, I went home three times to take care of my father. Not rushed visits squeezed between obligations but intentional time, creating memories, making sure he felt the love I carried for him. Not at his funeral, but in his life. While he was still here. While my presence could still matter.

In 2024, my father transitioned. My relationship ended. The fireballs life threw at me burned away the comfort I had built, the stability I had worked so hard to create. But they could not burn the woman I had become. She was fireproof by then. Forged in earlier flames. Unbreakable in ways that had nothing to do with being hard and everything to do with being rooted.

The Mirror My Partner Held Up

That man, the one who came into my life in 2022, he was not just a partner. He was a mirror. One of the clearest, most unflinching mirrors I have ever encountered.

He showed me the wounds I had buried under achievement, the ones I thought I had healed because I had simply stopped looking at them. He showed me the parts of me that still needed attention, the little girl who still flinched, the woman who still doubted, the heart that still braced for abandonment even in the midst of safety.

Not with criticism. Not with cruelty. But with love, patience, and honesty. He held space for my growth without trying to fix me. He reflected what I could not see on my own, trusting me to do the work of changing it.

I did not walk away bitter when it ended. I walked away better. More whole. More aware. More grateful for what we shared and what it taught me about myself.

For the first time in my life, I did not see a breakup as rejection. I saw it as a redirect. Not a door slammed in my face, but a path gently rerouted toward something even more aligned with who I was becoming. The ending was not a failure. It was a completion. A chapter closing so that the next one could begin.

The Deepest Lesson

This is what I learned, the lesson that runs beneath everything else:

You cannot manifest a life you are not emotionally available for. You can vision board all you want, recite affirmations until your voice goes hoarse, but if your internal landscape does not match what you are calling in, it will not stick. The opportunities might come, but you will not be able to receive them. The love might arrive, but you will sabotage it with old patterns. The success might find you, but you will feel like an imposter wearing someone else's clothes.

You cannot love others if you refuse to love yourself. Every relationship will become a mirror reflecting your own self-abandonment. Every connection will trigger the wounds you have been avoiding. You will attract what matches your internal state, not your external desires.

You cannot be present if you are still hiding from your past. The unprocessed pain will keep pulling you backward, stealing you from moments that deserve your full attention, keeping part of you locked in rooms you think you have left.

Self-love is not aesthetics. It is not face masks and bubble baths and Instagram captions about treating yourself. It is alignment. It is the daily choice to honor your needs. It is the ongoing work of healing what is broken. It is the courage to set boundaries and the wisdom to keep them.

When you raise your standards for how you treat yourself, everything around you rises to meet them. Your relationships improve because you stop tolerating what diminishes you. Your opportunities expand because you stop shrinking from what you deserve. Your faith deepens because you stop hiding from a God who already sees you completely. Your lifestyle shifts because you stop accepting less than what nourishes you. Your peace becomes unshakeable because it is no longer dependent on external validation.

The Rebirth

After the dust settled from 2024, after the grief and the endings and the stripping away, I wrote a new vision. Not from desperation this time. From clarity.

I saw the next five years unfolding: A new book that would help others walk the path I had walked. A podcast where I could share conversations that mattered. Relaunching my coaching program with the wisdom I had gained. Multiple streams of income that supported my purpose and my peace. More joy than I had ever allowed myself. More laughter, the deep kind that comes from a life well-lived. More softness, permission to be gentle with myself and the world. A circle of quality humans who saw me fully and loved me anyway. Love that felt like home, steady and safe and sacred. And a life that felt like mine.

Not borrowed from someone else's expectations. Not performed for approval. Not survived through gritted teeth and white-knuckled endurance. But lived. Fully. Freely. Faithfully.

Final Note

Everything did not happen at once. I want you to know that. There were no overnight transformations, no sudden arrivals at a destination that erased all the struggle of the journey. It unfolded piece by piece, day by day, choice by choice.

Not everything was easy. Some of it was the hardest work I have ever done. Some days I wanted to quit. Some nights I cried myself to sleep wondering if any of it would ever pay off.

Not everything stayed. Some of what I built fell apart. Some of what I loved walked away. Some of what I was certain about proved to be temporary.

But everything taught me. Every failure was a teacher. Every heartbreak was a curriculum. Every loss showed me that I was strong enough to survive.

To love myself better. To honor God deeper. To see myself clearly, without the distortion of old wounds and borrowed beliefs. To live with my heart open, even when it would be easier to close it.

And that, I have come to understand, is the greatest manifestation of all. Not the cars or the houses or the trips to tropical islands. But the woman who emerged from the fire. The one who finally learned to love herself. The one who stopped performing and started living. The one who chose truth over comfort and found that truth was the greatest comfort of all.

That woman is waiting for you too. She has been there all along, on the other side of your healing, ready to welcome you home.

~

Now, let us explore the roles we learned to play in order to be loved.

CHAPTER TWO

The Roles We Wear to Be Loved

"When you wear a mask long enough, even your reflection forgets your name."

We all play roles. We learn them so early and perform them so consistently that we forget they are performances at all. The Good Girl. The Fixer. The High Achiever. The Ride-or-Die. These are not personality types. They are survival strategies, carefully constructed identities designed to secure love in environments where love felt conditional, scarce, or dangerously unpredictable.

We learned early that love was not guaranteed. It had to be earned, managed, or maintained through constant vigilance and adjustment. Like a plant growing toward the only available light, we shaped ourselves toward whatever seemed to bring approval, affection, or at minimum, safety. And in that shaping, we lost pieces of ourselves we did not even know we were surrendering.

For many women, that training starts long before romance ever enters the picture. It begins in childhood living rooms and family dinner tables. It begins with the adults we watched and the conclusions we drew from their words and silences. We were praised for being "mature for our age," and we learned that our childhood was less important than adult comfort. We were called "selfless," and we learned that our needs should come last, if they should come at all. We were labeled "strong" and "independent," and we learned that needing help was weakness, that asking for support was burden.

But no one told us the cost. No one explained that strength without rest would eventually cost us softness. That people-pleasing was really just people-survival, a strategy born of necessity that would outlive its usefulness and become its own kind of prison. We learned to trade authenticity for approval and called it love. We learned to abandon ourselves in increments so small we barely noticed, until one day we woke up and could not remember who we were without the role.

The Good Girl Trap

She is polite. She is kind. She does not ask for much, and when she does, she apologizes for it. She has learned to take up as little space as possible, to smooth her edges, to anticipate needs before they are spoken, to make herself easy to love by making herself easy to overlook.

But underneath her composure is a quiet fear that runs like an underground river, invisible but always present. The fear whispers: "If I ask for what I need, they will think I am too demanding. Too needy. Too much. And they will leave." So she does not ask. She hints. She hopes. She waits for people to notice what she needs without her having to say it, and when they do not notice, she tells herself it does not matter anyway.

You know you are in the Good Girl trap when you feel a tightening in your chest at the thought of disappointing someone. When your stomach drops at the possibility of conflict. When you find yourself rehearsing conversations in your head, editing out anything that might make someone uncomfortable, even if that discomfort is the natural consequence of truth.

You tolerate discomfort and call it gratitude. You tell yourself you should be happy with what you have, even when what you have is not enough. You celebrate crumbs and call it humility. You convince yourself that wanting more is greedy, that your desires are excessive, that the ache in your heart is a character flaw rather than a legitimate need. You carry other people's emotions and call it empathy. You absorb their moods, manage their feelings, take responsibility for their comfort while neglecting your own.

But deep down, beneath all that accommodation, you are exhausted. You are tired in ways that sleep cannot fix. Because being "good" has become your prison, and the bars are made of everyone else's expectations.

You see, the Good Girl does not want to disappoint anyone. Not God. Not her family. Not her partner or her friends. She has built her entire identity around being the one people can count on, the one who never causes problems, the one who makes everything easier for everyone else. But in pleasing everyone, she forgets the woman she was before the world told her to smile and be nice. She loses touch with her own desires, her own opinions, her own voice.

Sometimes the Good Girl transforms into her shadow. When the pressure of constant accommodation becomes unbearable, she flips to the opposite extreme. She becomes tough, but not the kind of toughness that is empowering or inspiring. It is the kind that makes people fear her instead of respecting and admiring her. It is armor forged from suppressed resentment, a hardness that protects her from further hurt but also prevents her from receiving the softness she secretly craves.

Here is a hard truth: Being agreeable is not the same as being aligned. You can smile and nod and accommodate while your soul screams in protest.

And being bossy is not the same as being a leader. You can demand and control and micromanage while true authority, the kind that inspires rather than intimidates, remains out of reach. The goal is not to swing from one extreme to the other. The goal is to find the center, to be neither the pushover nor the tyrant, but the woman who knows her worth and lives from that knowing.

The Fixer and the Rescuer

Some women love like healers and suffer like martyrs and think it is a flex. They wear their exhaustion like a badge of honor, their sacrifice like a crown. They have turned self-abandonment into an art form and called it devotion.

We see potential in people and call it purpose. We look at someone who is broken, struggling, lost, and we feel a pull toward them that we mistake for destiny. We think: "I can help them. I can see who they could be if only someone believed in them enough." And we appoint ourselves as that believer, that savior, that bridge between who they are and who we imagine they could become.

We think if we just love harder, pray longer, stay stronger, they will change. Whether it is your parent who never gave you the love you needed, your partner who keeps promising to do better, or your boss who takes advantage of your dedication. We pour and pour and pour, convinced that our love is the missing ingredient, that our sacrifice will be the catalyst for their transformation.

The truth is harder to swallow: When you spend your life rescuing others, you drown in their storms. You become so focused on keeping them afloat that you do not notice you are sinking. Your needs become invisible, first to them and eventually to yourself. Your life becomes a series of emergencies that are never your own.

Love is not rehabilitation. It is partnership. Two whole people walking together, supporting each other, growing side by side. Not one person dragging another toward health while depleting her own. You cannot fix someone who benefits from staying broken. Some people have built their entire identity around their wounds. They receive attention, care, and accommodation because of their brokenness. To heal would mean losing the very thing that keeps others orbiting around them.

I once worked with a client I will call Lena. She was a brilliant woman in her forties, successful by every external measure, who had been in three long-term relationships, each with men who "needed" her help. She helped them get clean from addictions. She helped them get jobs when they were unemployed. She helped them get centered when they were lost. She poured her resources, her energy, her very life force into their healing. And every single time, once they did get better, they left.

One day, after another heartbreak, she sat across from me with tears streaming down her face and said something that changed everything: "I keep asking God to send me a healed man. But maybe He is asking me to stop trying to play God."

That was the day she stopped rescuing others and started rescuing herself. She realized that her attraction to broken men was not compassion. It was control. It was a way to feel needed, valuable, indispensable. As long as they needed her, they would not leave. Except they always did once they no longer needed what she was offering.

The High Achiever Who Feels Unseen

She has the degrees, the business, the followers, the image. From the outside, her life looks like a vision board come to life. She has built a life most people would envy, accumulated accomplishments that gleam like trophies on an invisible shelf. Yet she lies awake at night, staring at the ceiling, wondering: "Why does love feel so far? Why do I have everything except the one thing I want most?"

Because these great achievements are wonderful. They are evidence of discipline, intelligence, perseverance, and talent. But they cannot replace secure attachment. They cannot substitute for commitment and intimacy. You cannot accomplish your way into feeling loved. You cannot earn enough gold stars to quiet the part of you that still wonders if you are worthy of being chosen simply for who you are.

No matter how much success you accumulate, you cannot outwork an unhealed wound. The wound will simply find new expressions, new arenas in which to manifest. It will show up as perfectionism, as workaholism, as an inability to rest, as relationships that never quite satisfy because you are never quite present for them.

I know this woman. I was this woman for many years. I wore success like armor, hoping it would make rejection hurt less. I thought if I could just achieve enough, become impressive enough, accumulate enough evidence of my value, then I would finally feel safe. Then love would finally find me, attracted by my shine, convinced by my resume.

But no accomplishment can quiet the little girl who still wonders, "Was I ever enough when I was just me? Before the degrees and the titles and the accolades? When I had nothing to offer but my presence, was that presence ever enough?"

It took me years to understand that my worth was not in how much I could do. It was in how much of my true, authentic, feminine self I could keep while doing it. Achievement that costs you your essence is not success. It is a sophisticated form of self-abandonment, dressed up in external validation.

As Scripture reminds us: "What good is it for someone to gain the whole world, yet forfeit their soul?" (Mark 8:36) You can have everything and still have nothing if you have lost yourself in the getting.

The Ride-or-Die Myth

There is a version of love we have glorified in songs and movies and cultural narratives. The kind that endures chaos, disrespect, and disappointment in the name of "loyalty." We call it "holding it down." We call it "standing by your man." We call it love that weathers any storm, forgives any betrayal, endures any pain.

We think staying through pain is proof of strength. We think our capacity to absorb mistreatment demonstrates the depth of our commitment. We think leaving would be failure, would be weakness, would be proof that we did not love hard enough.

But loyalty without reciprocity is self-abandonment in disguise. It is not devotion. It is destruction, dressed up in noble language to make it more palatable. True loyalty is mutual. It is two people committed to each other's well-being, not one person sacrificing their well-being for someone who is not equally invested.

I remember once defending a man who consistently forgot my worth. I made excuses for his behavior. I explained away his neglect. I told my friends they did not understand the complexity of our relationship, the depth of what we shared. I thought if I could love him enough, he would remember to love me back. He would see what he had. He would change.

He did not. Because it is not your job to convince someone of your value. It is your job to believe it yourself, and then to align yourself with people who believe it too.

He had many things I had prayed for, at least aesthetically. He looked like the answer to prayers I had been whispering for years. But here is what I had to learn: I was not ready for what I prayed for. I had not made room for it. I had not done the internal work to receive what I was requesting. So I got what mirrored what I was hiding within. I attracted a reflection of my own unhealed places, my own unacknowledged wounds, my own secret belief that I did not truly deserve what I claimed to want.

When it ended, I blamed him for not appreciating the things I did. Things I realized later, he never asked me to do. I was giving from my own script, performing love the way I thought it should look, and then feeling resentful when he did not applaud a show he never requested. I told myself, "I was just trying to help." But I was not ready to take accountability for the part I played in creating a dynamic that could never satisfy either of us.

Now I simply appreciate the part he played in my journey of life. He was not a villain. He was a teacher, showing me through his presence what I still needed to learn about myself.

The Mask of Strength

For many women, "strong" is a survival mechanism, not a personality trait. It is armor forged in necessity, protection developed in environments where vulnerability was dangerous, where showing weakness invited exploitation or abandonment.

We say, "I'm fine," when we are falling apart. We say, "I got it," when we are drowning. We say, "I don't need anyone," when we are aching for someone to see through the performance and offer help we cannot bring ourselves to ask for.

But behind that armor is a soft heart. One that still longs to exhale, to put down the weight, to be held without having to hold everything together first. One that still hopes someone will be strong enough to receive her vulnerability, safe enough to trust with her tenderness.

How do you know if strength has become a mask? Pay attention to your body. Notice if you tense when someone offers help. Notice if you deflect compliments, dismiss care, or minimize your own needs. Notice if there is a part of you that feels relieved when people do not get too close, even as another part aches from the distance.

Strength has its place. It has gotten you through situations that would have broken others. It has protected you when protection was necessary. But when strength becomes a wall instead of a boundary, when it keeps out danger but also keeps out love, you end up living behind it, safe but alone, protected but untouched.

The truth is: You can be strong and still need softness. You can be independent and still crave intimacy. You can be powerful and still long to be protected. These are not contradictions. They are the full spectrum of what it means to be human. A woman's strength is not meant to compete with a man's. It is meant to complement his, to create something together that neither could create alone. They are meant to be interdependent, each bringing what the other needs, both whole on their own but more together.

The woman who learns to rest in her softness becomes more powerful than the woman still trying to prove her strength. Because true power does not need to announce itself. It does not need constant demonstration. It simply is, quietly confident, securely rooted, at peace with itself.

When I Forgot My Name

Let me tell you about a moment that crystallized everything I am trying to share. Years ago, I was leading a delegation in the Sahel region of Africa. There were six men on the team, all powerful, respected leaders in their fields. I was the only woman. I had earned my place at that table through years of work, expertise, and demonstrated capability. But not everyone saw it that way.

One afternoon, we were sitting in a conference room, waiting for our host to join us. The room was formal, all polished wood and leather chairs, the kind of space designed to communicate importance. I was reviewing my notes when one of the local associates approached me. He handed me several bottles of water and gestured toward the men seated around the table, indicating that I should serve them.

At first, I smiled, thinking it was perhaps a cultural misunderstanding, a moment of harmless hospitality. Maybe he did not realize I was part of the delegation. I set the bottles aside and returned to my notes. But it happened again. And again. Each time with the unspoken assumption that of course the woman would serve, regardless of her title or role.

That is when I realized it was not an accident. It was not a misunderstanding. They did not see a leader. They saw a woman. And in their framework, those two things could not occupy the same space.

I remember sitting quietly, feeling the fire rise in my chest. That familiar battle between pride and peace. Between righteous anger and strategic wisdom. Part of me wanted to stand up and announce my credentials, to demand recognition, to make a scene that would ensure no one forgot who I was again. Another part of me knew that approach would cost more than it would gain, that there was a more effective way to address the situation.

I whispered a prayer, asking for guidance, for the right words, for the grace to handle this moment in a way I would be proud of later. Then I leaned over to one of my partners, a managing director who understood my position, and told him quietly what I had observed. He handled it with grace and respect, addressing the team in a way that corrected the assumption without shaming anyone.

That day reminded me of something important: Being feminine does not make you less capable. Your gender is not a liability to be overcome or a limitation to be apologized for. But it does invite you to lead differently. With grace, not aggression. With power, not performance. With the kind of authority that does not need to dominate to be respected.

True equality is not imitation. It is not about becoming a woman-shaped version of a man. It is integration. It is bringing your full self, including your femininity, to every space you occupy, and trusting that your presence adds something that could not exist without you.

A Modern Reflection on Feminine Power

Society tells us that equality means "doing what men do." Success is measured by masculine metrics: aggression, dominance, competition, conquest. We are taught to lean in, to fight harder, to leave our softness at the door if we want to be taken seriously.

But divine femininity says something different: "I bring what only I can bring, and I deserve equal respect, equal pay, and equal opportunity." Not because I can do what a man does, but because what I do is equally valuable. Different is not lesser. Feminine is not weaker. It is simply another expression of strength, another pathway to power, another way of moving through the world that has been devalued for too long.

Your nurturing nature is not a weakness to be managed. Your intuition is not irrationality to be dismissed. Your ability to sense truth in silence, to read what is unspoken, to know things before they can be proven, that is power. I call it "Quiet Power." It can be healing, and it can also be lethal. The kind of feminine power that can take a man from commoner to king, or vice versa. The kind that is felt before it is seen, that shifts the energy of a room simply by entering it.

You do not need to be "a man in heels" to be respected. You do not need to harden yourself, to strip away your tenderness, to apologize for your emotions. A real man does not compete with your light. He covers it, protects it, creates conditions where it can shine brighter than it ever could alone.

And when a woman feels emotionally safe, when she knows she is held and protected and valued, she does not lose her independence. She becomes more luminous. More herself. More powerful in ways that have nothing to do with force and everything to do with presence. That is her superpower, the radiance that emerges when the goddess within feels safe enough to show herself.

Because submission, when healthy, is not surrender. It is trust. It is the choice to let someone lead in areas where their leadership serves you both. It is not weakness. It is wisdom, knowing when to hold on and when to let go, when to push forward and when to allow yourself to be carried.

Spiritual Truth

God did not design you to be everything for everyone. He did not create you to pour out endlessly without ever being refilled. He did not intend for you to sacrifice yourself on the altar of other people's needs while your own needs go perpetually unmet.

Even Jesus withdrew from the crowd to pray. Even the Savior of the world needed solitude, rest, communion with the Father. "Come away by yourselves to a secluded place and rest a while." (Mark 6:31) This was not weakness. This was wisdom. This was modeling for us what sustainable love actually looks like.

If the Savior of the world needed rest, so do you. If He needed to step away from the demands of others to reconnect with His source, so do you. If He needed boundaries between Himself and the endless needs of those around Him, so do you.

Your worth is not in what you give. It is in who you are when you finally stop giving everything away. When the performances end. When the roles are set aside. When you stand before God and yourself with nothing to offer but your presence. That is when you discover what was always true: you were enough before you did anything at all.

Hard Truths

The more you perform, the less you are seen. Every mask you wear is a barrier between you and genuine connection. People may love your performance, but that is not the same as loving you.

You cannot be chosen while pretending to be someone else. If you have to be inauthentic to be loved, then it is not you who is loved. It is a character you created, a role you play. And maintaining that character is exhausting work that yields counterfeit rewards.

If love requires you to betray yourself, it is not love. It is a contract of survival. It is a transaction where you trade pieces of your soul for the illusion of security. But that security is built on sand, and it will eventually collapse.

Your peace is not negotiable. It is not a luxury to be enjoyed only when everything else is handled. It is the foundation from which everything else should be built. Guard it fiercely.

Journal Prompts

> *What mask or role have I worn to feel safe or loved? When did I first learn to wear it? What was happening in my life when this mask became necessary?*
>
> *What would happen if I stopped performing and simply showed up as myself? What am I afraid would be revealed? What am I afraid I would lose?*
>
> *What version of me am I most afraid to reveal, and why? What would it take to show that version to someone I trust?*
>
> *How does my body feel when I am performing versus when I am being authentic? What physical sensations tell me the truth about which mode I am in?*

Affirmation

I no longer perform to be loved. I am enough in my truth, my softness, and my wholeness. I am safe, loved, and supported at my worst and at my best. The roles I played kept me surviving. The woman I am becoming will help me thrive.

Closing Truth

Every time you drop a mask, you become more magnetic to the kind of love that sees you, desires you, and values you. Not the performance. Not the role. You. The woman behind all the adaptations, the one who has been waiting to be discovered underneath everything she learned to become.

The woman you are becoming does not need to perform. She does not need to prove. She does not need to earn her place at any table. She just needs to be. Fully, unapologetically, authentically herself.

Because the one who truly loves you will never ask you to shrink to fit their vision. They will not need you to edit yourself, to dim your light, to become smaller so they can feel larger. They will expand to meet your truth. They will rise to match your wholeness. They will love you not despite who you really are, but because of it.

And that love, when it comes, will feel like nothing you have ever experienced. Because you will finally be present to receive it with no mask between you and the gift being offered.

~

Now that we understand the roles we have played, let us explore why we keep repeating the patterns that broke us.

CHAPTER THREE

Why We Repeat What Broke Us

"Until you heal the wound, the pattern will feel like fate."

The Hidden Blueprint

Painful patterns do not start with partners. They start with programming. Long before you ever held someone's hand or felt your heart race at the sound of a particular voice, you were being shaped. Molded. Taught what love looked like, even if no one ever sat you down and explained it directly.

We were all shaped by the environments that raised us. The tone of our parents' voices when they spoke to each other, and when they spoke to us. The silences in our homes, heavy with things unsaid, conflicts unresolved, emotions unexpressed. The way love was given, whether freely or conditionally, consistently or in unpredictable bursts. And perhaps most powerfully, the way love was withheld, the moments when we reached for connection and found absence instead.

These early experiences wrote themselves into our bodies like code into a computer. They created templates, blueprints, unconscious instructions that would run in the background of every relationship we would ever enter. And the most insidious part? We did not know they were there. We thought we were making free choices. We thought we were following our hearts. But we were following a map drawn by someone else, navigating by stars that had been placed in our sky before we were old enough to question their arrangement.

If love looked like chaos in your childhood home, you will chase adrenaline and call it passion. The calm, steady presence of a healthy partner will feel boring, lifeless, missing something essential. You will find yourself drawn instead to the ones who keep you guessing, who run hot and cold, who make your heart race with uncertainty rather than safety.

If love sounded like criticism, if affection came wrapped in correction, if you were loved through being improved rather than accepted, you will call peace "boring." You will feel uncomfortable with someone who simply appreciates you as you are. Part of you will be waiting for the other shoe to drop, for the critique that proves they are really paying attention.

If love felt like walking on eggshells, if you learned to read moods and adjust yourself accordingly, if you became an expert at managing someone else's emotions to keep yourself safe, you will find comfort in tension. Ease will feel unfamiliar, almost suspicious. You will not know what to do with yourself when there is no crisis to manage, no mood to navigate, no emotional fire to put out.

I used to think I just had "bad luck" in love. That was the story I told myself, the explanation that required no deeper examination. Same story, different face. Different birthdays, different names, but the same heartbreak playing on repeat like a song I could not stop hearing.

It was not bad luck. It was the body's way of trying to resolve what the heart refused to release. My unconscious mind was seeking out situations that matched my original wound, hoping that this time, with this person, I could finally get it right. I could finally earn the love that had once been withheld. I could finally prove I was worthy of what had always seemed just out of reach.

Because here is the truth that changed everything for me: You do not attract what you want. You attract what feels familiar. And familiar is not always safe. Sometimes, it is just what your nervous system recognizes as home. Your body seeks what it knows, even when what it knows was painful, because at least pain that is predictable feels manageable. At least the devil you know seems less frightening than the angel you have never met.

That is not dysfunction. That is conditioning. That is a survival mechanism that once served you, doing its job long after the job became obsolete. Your nervous system is not trying to hurt you. It is trying to protect you using the only tools it was given.

But God never intended your childhood lessons to become your adult limitations. The patterns that helped you survive your family of origin were not meant to define every relationship for the rest of your life. They were adaptations, temporary measures, scaffolding that was always meant to come down once the building was complete.

The Woman Who Called Chaos "Chemistry"

Maya grew up in a home where conflict was constant. The walls of her childhood absorbed shouting matches and slammed doors, tears and accusations, love expressed through intensity rather than consistency. Her parents loved her, there was no doubt about that, but their affection came in bursts. Unpredictable. Conditional. One moment overwhelming warmth, the next cold withdrawal. She never knew which version of love she would receive on any given day.

So when she started dating as an adult, her body only felt "alive" when things were unstable. That jolt of adrenaline, that heightened awareness, that sense of being on the edge of something, that was what her nervous system had learned to associate with love. Without the chaos, everything felt flat. Empty. Like something essential was missing.

If a man was consistent, she would somehow lose interest. She always had a justified excuse, of course. He was too nice. There was no spark. She just was not feeling it. But the truth was that his steadiness felt foreign to her body, and foreign felt wrong, even when it was healthy.

If he was distant, she would chase harder, calling it effort. Calling it not giving up. Calling it the kind of dedication that real love required. She did not recognize that she was simply replaying the dynamic she had learned in childhood: reach for love, find it elusive, try harder, reach again.

If he criticized her, she would overperform. She would work tirelessly to show him she could be good, she could be better, she could be worthy of approval. The criticism felt familiar. It felt like a language she already spoke fluently. Acceptance without conditions felt like a foreign tongue she did not trust herself to translate.

When her therapist asked, "When did you first feel this kind of excitement?" something shifted in Maya. She sat with the question, really sat with it, and followed the feeling backward through time. And she realized the truth: It was not exciting. It was anxiety. Her nervous system had mistaken survival for love. What she called butterflies were actually alarm bells. What she called passion was actually fear dressed up in more romantic clothing.

When she began to heal, when she started doing the deep work of understanding her patterns and retraining her responses, she said something that stayed with me long after our conversation ended: "I realized I didn't want butterflies anymore. I wanted peace."

That is when her relationships began to change. Not because the men changed, not because she suddenly started meeting better people, but because she finally stopped negotiating her peace for attention. She stopped mistaking chaos for chemistry. She stopped accepting anxiety as the price of admission to love.

Why the Pattern Feels Like Fate

You can leave the person. You can change your number. You can block the contact, delete the photos, move to a different city, and promise yourself that this time will be different. But if you do not heal the wound, you will meet them again. Different face. Different name. Same soul lesson wrapped in new packaging.

The cycle repeats until awareness interrupts it. Until you stop running from relationship to relationship and stand still long enough to examine what you are carrying. Until you stop asking "Why do I keep meeting the wrong people?" but "Why do the wrong people feel so right to me?".

We do not repeat patterns because we are foolish. We are not stupid for finding ourselves in the same situation again and again. We repeat them because we are seeking redemption in the same places we were once wounded. Some part of us believes that if we can just get it right this time, with this person who reminds us of the one who first hurt us, we can finally heal that original wound. We can prove we were worthy all along. We can rewrite the ending of a story that was written before we had any say in it.

The child who felt unseen keeps picking emotionally unavailable partners, hoping that this time her love will be enough to make someone turn toward her, to make someone finally see her the way she always longed to be seen.

The one who felt responsible for everyone's happiness keeps attracting people who need saving, hoping that this time her sacrifice will be rewarded, that her devotion will finally earn her the reciprocal care she has always given freely.

The one who grew up around inconsistency confuses chaos for chemistry, mistaking the familiar surge of anxiety for the unfamiliar warmth of genuine connection.

You are not addicted to pain. You are addicted to what feels familiar. And there is an important difference there. Pain is not what you are seeking.

Familiarity is. Your nervous system is simply doing what nervous systems do: gravitating toward what it recognizes, what it has already mapped, what it knows how to navigate even when the navigation is exhausting.

But familiarity is not destiny. It is just programming. And programming can be rewritten. Neural pathways that were laid down in childhood can be redirected in adulthood. Patterns that feel inevitable can be interrupted, examined, and transformed. You are not stuck. You are just repeating what you have not yet understood.

The Repetition Loop

Let me walk you through how the cycle typically unfolds. Understanding the stages can help you recognize where you are in the pattern and where intervention becomes possible.

Stage One: Attraction. The thrill, the rush, the "click." You are googly-eyed, intoxicated by possibility. This person feels different. Special. Like they understand you in ways no one else ever has. Your body lights up in their presence. Every conversation feels electric. You cannot stop thinking about them.

Stage Two: Attachment. The fantasy begins to take shape. They feel like home, and you tell yourself this is the one. You start imagining a future together. You overlook small concerns because the larger picture seems so promising. You invest emotionally, opening yourself in ways that feel vulnerable and exciting.

Stage Three: Discomfort. You start noticing red flags. Behaviors that do not quite sit right. Patterns that remind you of past pain. But you rationalize them. You tell yourself it is not that bad. You explain away your own concerns. You silence the inner voice that knows something is off because you have already invested so much, and the fantasy is so beautiful, and surely it will get better.

Stage Four: Conflict. You overgive, trying to fix what feels broken. You overexplain, hoping that if you just communicate clearly enough, they will finally understand. You overstay, convinced that your persistence will be rewarded, that your love will be the thing that changes everything. The relationship becomes work, but you tell yourself that all relationships require effort.

Stage Five: Collapse. You leave, or they do. The ending arrives, whether suddenly or gradually. You are left processing what happened, grieving what you hoped it would become, wondering what you could have done differently.

Stage Six: Repeat. You promise to choose better next time. You tell yourself you have learned your lesson. And then you meet someone new, and they feel "different," and the cycle begins again. The same story unfolds with new characters, and you wonder why you cannot seem to break free.

Healing happens when you finally pause between stages three and four. When you notice the discomfort and, instead of rationalizing it away, you sit with it. You ask not "Why are they like this?" but "Why does this feel normal to me? Why am I willing to accept this? What wound is being activated that makes this pattern feel familiar?"

Interrupting the Loop: A Practical Exercise

When you recognize you are in stage three or four of the loop, when you feel that familiar pull toward overgiving, overexplaining, or overstaying, here is a practice that can interrupt the pattern:

First, pause physically. Stop what you are doing. Put down your phone. Step away from the conversation, even if just mentally. Create space between the trigger and your response.

Second, place your hand on your heart. Feel its rhythm. This physical gesture activates your parasympathetic nervous system and reminds your body that you are safe in this moment, right here, right now.

Third, ask yourself three questions: "How old do I feel right now?" Often, when we are triggered, we are responding from a younger version of ourselves, the child who first learned this pattern. Naming the age can help you recognize what is happening. Then ask: "What does this younger me need to hear?" Speak to that younger self with the compassion you would offer a frightened child. Finally: "What would the healed version of me do in this moment?" Let that question guide your next action.

Fourth, delay your response. You do not have to react immediately. You can say, "I need some time to think about this." You can wait before sending that text. You can sleep on a decision. The pattern wants urgency. Healing lives in the pause.

This is not about perfection. You will not interrupt every loop every time. But each time you catch yourself, each time you pause instead of reacting automatically, you are building new neural pathways. You are teaching your nervous system that there is another way.

The Woman Who Finally Chose Different

I once mentored a woman named Sarah who had just left a man who drained her emotionally. She came to me exhausted, depleted, wondering if she would ever break free of the pattern that had defined her romantic life for two decades.

She said, "Every time I try to move on, I meet another version of him. Different job, different name, different face. But the same dynamic. The same drain. The same ending."

I told her gently, "That's because your healing isn't complete. It's just relocated. You've been changing your external circumstances without changing your internal programming. You've been switching partners without switching patterns."

So we did the inner work. Deep work. Uncomfortable work. We started re-parenting her inner child, that part of her that had learned love meant depletion, that being chosen meant being drained. She began journaling every time she felt "chemistry," not to celebrate it but to examine it. What was this feeling, really? Where had she felt it before? What pattern was it connected to?

Instead of asking, "Does he like me?" she started asking, "Do I feel safe?" Instead of wondering if she was enough for him, she started wondering if he was safe for her. The questions themselves began to rewire her approach.

Six months later, she met someone steady. Ready. Intentional. A man who did not keep her guessing, who did not require her to decode mixed signals, who showed up consistently and communicated clearly.

At first, she said, "I'm not sure if I'm attracted to him. There's no spark." I asked her to sit with that observation instead of acting on it. To notice what her body was actually experiencing when she was with him. To pay attention to what might be hiding beneath that label of "no spark."

After a few weeks, she realized what she had mistaken for boredom was peace. What she had interpreted as lack of chemistry was actually the absence of anxiety. Her nervous system was not firing its usual alarms because there was nothing to be alarmed about. The quiet she felt was not the quiet of disconnection. It was the quiet of safety.

That is what healing does. It changes your taste. It rewires your attraction. When those old patterns are finally updated, when the programming is rewritten, what once felt exciting starts to feel exhausting, and what once felt boring starts to feel like home.

The Reprogramming Process

You cannot will your way out of emotional habits. You cannot simply decide to be attracted to different people and have it magically work. The patterns live deeper than conscious thought. They live in your nervous system, in your body's automatic responses, in the split-second judgments your brain makes before your conscious mind even registers what is happening.

You must retrain your nervous system. You must teach it, through repeated experience, that safety is survivable. That calm is not boring but beautiful. That consistency is not the absence of passion but the presence of trustworthiness.

This means choosing people who feel peaceful, even when part of you whispers that they seem "too calm." Even when your nervous system is scanning for the familiar chaos and not finding it. Trust that the discomfort you feel in their presence might be the discomfort of growth, not the discomfort of incompatibility.

This means saying no to drama, even when it feels tempting. Even when that part of you that was raised in chaos starts to feel restless and bored. Recognize the restlessness for what it is: withdrawal from a familiar drug, not evidence that something is wrong.

This means practicing safety through stillness. Through prayer that quiets the noise. Through breathwork that regulates your nervous system. Through journaling that helps you process rather than suppress. Through solitude that teaches you that you are enough company for yourself.

This means rewarding yourself for leaving chaos early, not for surviving it longer. The badge of honor should be how quickly you recognized the pattern and stepped away, not how much pain you endured before finally letting go.

Healing is not about avoiding love. It is about recognizing when love is real. It is about developing the discernment to know the difference between what feels familiar and what is actually good for you. It is about trusting yourself to choose wisely, even when wise choices feel foreign at first.

Psychology Meets Spirit

Dr. Joe Dispenza once said, "You can't create a new future while holding on to the emotions of the past."

This is not just psychological truth. It is spiritual truth. The two are more connected than we often realize.

You cannot pray for divine love while clinging to relationships that dishonor your worth. You cannot ask God for a healthy partnership while accepting treatment that degrades your soul. The prayer and the tolerance cannot coexist indefinitely. Something has to give.

You cannot receive God's peace while entertaining what keeps your nervous system in constant warfare. If your relationships feel like battlegrounds, if you are always bracing for the next conflict, always managing someone else's volatility, you are not in a position to receive the rest that has been promised to you.

Every healed choice you make becomes a new prayer in motion. When you walk away from chaos, that is worship. When you choose peace over passion, that is faith. When you trust that what feels unfamiliar might actually be what is healthy, that is surrender to a God who knows better than your conditioning what love is supposed to feel like.

The Apostle Paul wrote: "Do not be conformed to the pattern of this world, but be transformed by the renewing of your mind." (Romans 12:2)

This is not just about faith in an abstract sense. It is about emotional reprogramming. It is about the daily, practical work of changing how you think, how you respond, how you choose. Renewing your mind means teaching your soul that struggle is not a synonym for love. That pain is not proof of depth. That difficulty is not destiny.

Transformation begins when your truth feels safer than tension. When honesty becomes more comfortable than performance. When you no longer need the drama to feel alive because you have discovered that real aliveness comes from alignment, not anxiety.

Hard Truths

You cannot build a future on unhealed patterns. The foundation will always be unstable. No matter how beautiful the structure you try to build, it will keep crumbling if the ground beneath it is fractured.

Peace will feel "boring" until you have lived through enough chaos to recognize it as the gift it truly is. Until you have been exhausted enough, depleted enough, broken down enough by the drama you once craved, you will not appreciate the beauty of calm.

The love that feels unfamiliar might be the love that is healthy. Do not dismiss it simply because your nervous system does not recognize it. Be curious about what you are experiencing instead of immediately labeling it as wrong.

You cannot receive what you do not believe you deserve. Your internal sense of worthiness acts as a filter, letting in only what matches your self-concept. Expand your sense of deserving, and you expand what you are able to receive.

The pattern ends the moment you decide your peace is worth more than your pain. When you stop trading serenity for stimulation. When you stop accepting chaos as the cost of connection. When you finally declare that you are done participating in dynamics that diminish you.

Journal Prompts

> *What kind of love feels "safe" to me, and where did I first learn that? What was happening in my childhood home that taught me to associate certain dynamics with love?*
>
> *When I think of peace in a relationship, does it feel calming or uncomfortable? What does my body do when I imagine being with someone completely steady and consistent?*
>
> *What part of my past am I still trying to redeem through love? What wound am I hoping a partner will finally heal? What ending am I trying to rewrite?*

When I feel intense "chemistry," what is my body actually experiencing? Is it excitement, or is it anxiety in disguise?

Affirmation

I am not my past. I am safe to choose peace over patterns, calm over chaos, and truth over trauma. My history shaped me, but it does not define me. I am capable of new choices and new outcomes.

Closing Truth

You are not cursed. You are conditioned. And conditioning can be changed. The patterns that feel like fate are simply neural pathways that were laid down when you had no choice, when you were too young to question what you were learning, when survival required you to adapt in whatever ways were available to you.

You are not broken. You are awakening. Every time you recognize a pattern, you weaken its hold on you. Every time you pause before reacting, you create space for a different choice. Every time you choose differently, even when it feels strange, even when your nervous system protests, you are teaching your body a new language of love.

It will not always be easy. Sometimes your old self will crave the drama that once defined you. You will feel the pull toward what is familiar, the itch for chaos when life gets too calm. That is normal.

That is the old programming trying to reassert itself. Notice it without obeying it. Acknowledge it without acting on it.

Every healed "no" is a seed of freedom. Every time you walk away from what you once would have tolerated, you are planting something new. Every boundary you hold is evidence of growth. Every pattern you interrupt is a victory worth celebrating.

You are not repeating the past. You are rewriting it. One choice at a time. One day at a time. One relationship at a time. And when you finally learn the difference between love and survival, when you can feel in your body the distinction between genuine connection and familiar chaos, you will never mistake struggle for destiny again.

The woman you are becoming knows the difference. She is waiting for you to catch up to her. And she is patient, because she knows you are worth the wait.

~

Now that we understand why patterns repeat, let us discover the love that has been waiting for us all along: the love within ourselves.

CHAPTER FOUR

I Am the Love I've Been Waiting For

"You are not too much. You are just not meant to be consumed in pieces."

There comes a moment in every woman's journey when something shifts. It is not dramatic, not accompanied by fireworks or fanfare. It is quieter than that, more internal. A settling. A knowing. The moment when you stop waiting for someone to love you the way you need to be loved, because you realize you have been the answer all along.

The search ends. Not because you have given up, but because you have arrived. The striving softens. Not because you have lowered your standards, but because you no longer need external validation to know your worth. And you finally exhale into the most peaceful truth of all: you are the love you have been waiting for.

This is not arrogance. This is not the closing off of your heart to partnership. This is the opening of your heart to yourself, which is the prerequisite to opening it fully to anyone else. You cannot give what you do not have. You cannot receive what you do not believe you deserve. And you cannot build lasting love with another person if you have not first built it within yourself.

You stop auditioning for affection, performing versions of yourself designed to be palatable, acceptable, chosen. You stop explaining your worth to people who should recognize it without explanation. You stop shrinking, dimming, editing, apologizing for the space you occupy in this world.

You start living like a woman who knows. Who knows her own rhythm and honors it. Who knows her own radiance and lets it shine without apology. Who knows her own need for rest and takes it without guilt. These become her love language to herself, and from that place of fullness, real love finds her. Not because she is looking for it, but because she has become the frequency it recognizes.

The Awakening: From Performing to Being

When you begin to love yourself, truly love yourself in a way that is not performative or conditional, you do not become selfish. You become sane. You become clear. You become grounded in a way that allows you to give more generously, not less, because you are giving from overflow rather than depletion.

You stop negotiating with confusion, accepting mixed signals as complexity, translating inconsistency as depth. You stop rescuing chaos, no longer drawn to situations that need fixing, people who need saving, dynamics that require constant management. You stop mistaking attention for intimacy, understanding finally that someone noticing you is not the same as someone knowing you.

You realize truths that once would have felt like losses but now feel like liberation:

Love does not chase. It attracts and chooses. The right love does not require pursuit, convincing, or constant effort to maintain. It recognizes you and moves toward you with intention.

Peace does not need to announce itself. It is patient and preserves. Real peace does not require social media validation or external witnesses. It simply exists, quietly sustaining what is real.

Consistency is not a promise made in heated moments. It is a lifestyle, a daily practice, a thousand small choices that add up to trustworthiness.

Some women fear this awakening will make them lonely. They worry that raising their standards will shrink their options, that refusing to perform will leave them without an audience. But what this awakening actually does is refine their circle. It acts as a filter, separating those who were attracted to the performance from those who are drawn to the person.

When a woman stops performing for love, the wrong men lose interest. They drift away, confused by her stillness, uncomfortable with her clarity, uninterested in someone they cannot decode or chase. And in that space, the right one steps forward. The one who was waiting for her to stop running so he could find her. The one who does not need the performance because he wants the person.

What Choosing Yourself Actually Looks Like

"Choosing yourself" sounds beautiful in theory, but what does it actually mean in practice? What does it look like on a Tuesday afternoon when you are tempted to text the ex who just posted something that felt pointed? What does it look like on a Friday night when loneliness feels louder than conviction? What does it look like in the thousand small moments that add up to a life?

Choosing yourself looks like putting down the phone instead of sending that message you will regret. It looks like sitting with the discomfort of silence instead of filling it with someone who does not deserve your attention. It looks like letting the urge to reach out pass through you like a wave, trusting that it will crest and recede if you do not act on it.

Choosing yourself looks like going to bed at a reasonable hour instead of staying up scrolling through social media, comparing your life to highlight reels that do not show the full picture. It looks like drinking enough water, eating food that nourishes you, moving your body in ways that feel like celebration rather than punishment.

Choosing yourself looks like declining the invitation that would drain you, even when you feel guilty for saying no. It looks like canceling plans when you realize you made them from obligation rather than desire. It looks like protecting your energy as fiercely as you would protect a child in your care.

Choosing yourself looks like setting the boundary with the family member who always leaves you depleted, even though you know they will be hurt. It looks like having the difficult conversation instead of letting resentment build. It looks like speaking your truth even when your voice shakes, even when you are afraid of the response.

Choosing yourself looks like staying home on a Saturday night because solitude sounds better than settling for company that does not nourish you. It looks like taking yourself on dates, to restaurants and movies and museums, treating your own company as valuable, as enough.

Choosing yourself looks like walking away from the argument you know you could win but that is not worth the cost of winning. It looks like letting someone be wrong about you rather than exhausting yourself trying to change their perception. It looks like protecting your peace even when your pride wants to fight.

Choosing yourself looks like asking for what you need in relationships, directly and without apology, trusting that the right people will want to meet those needs. It looks like accepting nothing less than what you would tell your best friend to accept. It looks like treating your future self as someone worth protecting.

Every day is filled with these small opportunities to choose yourself or abandon yourself. Each one matters. Each one is practice. Each one is teaching your nervous system that you are trustworthy, that you will show up for yourself, that you will not betray your own well-being for temporary comfort or external approval.

When She Finally Met Herself

Tracy was thirty-six when she stopped trying to "fix" her love life and started fixing her mornings. It seemed like such a small shift, such an inconsequential change in focus. But it turned out to be everything.

She had spent years analyzing her patterns, reading relationship books, going on dates with renewed determination, adjusting her profile, trying different approaches. All of it focused outward. All of it assuming that the solution would come from outside herself, from finding the right person, the right strategy, the right combination of words and behaviors that would finally unlock lasting love.

Then something shifted. She stopped looking outward and started looking inward. She made her bed every morning, a simple act of honoring her space and her day. She made her tea, a ritual of presence and self-care. She prayed, connecting with something larger than her loneliness. She went for walks and hikes, moving her body through nature, feeling alive in ways that had nothing to do with another person. She loved hiking, the way it made her feel strong and capable, the way the trail demanded nothing but her presence.

And every day, she wrote down one sentence in her journal:

"I am the woman I once begged someone else to see."

At first, she did not believe it. The words felt like aspiration, not truth. But she wrote them anyway. Day after day. Week after week. And slowly, almost imperceptibly, something began to change. The words started to feel true. She started to see herself the way she had always wanted to be seen.

Not because anyone else had changed their perception, but because she had changed her own.

Six months later, she said something that struck me deeply: "I didn't find love. Love found me when I stopped hiding from myself."

When she met her partner, a calm, grounded man who saw her spirit before her beauty, she did not doubt him. She did not question his intentions or wait for the other shoe to drop. She did not second-guess his consistency or wonder when the "real" him would emerge. Because she already trusted herself. She trusted her own judgment, her own discernment, her own ability to recognize what was real.

He did not complete her. That is the important part. She was already complete. He met her whole. Two full people coming together, not to fill each other's gaps, but to share their abundance. Not to heal each other's wounds, but to walk alongside each other's healing. Not to become one, but to remain two who had chosen to build together.

What Healed Men Know

There are men who love deeply, quietly, and truthfully. They exist, these men, even though the loudest voices often belong to those who love poorly. They are not trending on social media. They are not building platforms on relationship advice. They are not performing masculinity for an audience. But they are loud in prayer, loud in action, loud in the ways that matter when no one is watching.

These men do not perform for power. They do not need to dominate to feel masculine, control to feel strong, or diminish others to feel large. They have done their own work. They have faced their own wounds. They have healed their egos enough to understand a profound truth: A woman's softness is not weakness. It is sacred energy that deserves stewardship, not control. Protection, not exploitation.

A healed man knows that respect is his "I love you." Not just the words, but the way he treats her time, her opinions, her boundaries, her dreams. Every act of respect is a declaration of love.

A healed man knows that presence is his poetry. He does not need elaborate words or grand gestures. His attention, his full attention, is the gift. His willingness to be there, fully there, without distraction or agenda, is the romance.

A healed man knows that safety is his offering. Not just physical safety, though that too, but emotional safety. The kind that allows her to exhale. The kind that creates space for her truth. The kind that does not punish vulnerability but honors it.

He does not compete with her light. He understands that her shine does not diminish his own, that there is no scarcity of radiance, that two people can both be luminous without one having to dim. He covers her light, not to snuff it out, but to protect it. To create the conditions where it can burn even brighter.

He does not need her to shrink. A healed man is not threatened by a woman's success, her intelligence, her ambition, her strength. He does not need to be the biggest thing in the room. He rises with her, not against her. He celebrates her expansion rather than fearing it.

When a man loves from wholeness, when he has done his own healing and comes to partnership from fullness rather than emptiness, he does not try to own you. He honors you. He does not try to possess you. He partners with you. He does not need you to complete him. He chooses you because you complement what is already whole.

Quiet Love

You will not see their names trending. They are not curating "relationship goals" content for strangers to consume. They are not performing their partnership for public consumption. Because real love is not public validation. It is private evolution. It is two people growing together in ways that do not require an audience.

Most couples who are truly aligned do not perform their love online. They are too busy living it. They live it through small gestures, the coffee made without asking, the hand on the back during a hard conversation, the laughter over inside jokes that no one else would understand. They live it through prayer, both together and for each other. They live it through emotional safety, the trust that allows them to bring their full selves into the relationship without fear.

They are not trying to prove love. They are too busy protecting it. Too busy nurturing it. Too busy tending to something real to waste energy convincing strangers it exists.

Social media has glamorized the appearance of romance. The trips to exotic locations. The matching outfits and coordinated aesthetics. The captions that read like poetry. But chemistry without character collapses with time. The spark that photographs well is not the same as the flame that keeps burning through difficulty, disappointment, and the long ordinary stretches of life that no one posts about.

What makes love last is simpler and less photogenic: truth, friendship, and peace. The willingness to be honest even when it is uncomfortable. The foundation of genuine friendship that remains when romantic feelings ebb and flow. The commitment to peace in a compassionate and forgiving way, choosing harmony over being right, choosing understanding over winning.

The quiet kind of love makes you forget to post because you are present. You are so absorbed in the moment, so nourished by what is actually happening, that the thought of documenting it for others does not even occur to you. The experience itself is enough.

Esther Perel, the renowned therapist, speaks of how love that used to be distributed across a family, a community, a network of friends, is now expected from one person. We expect our partner to be our best friend, our passionate lover, our intellectual equal, our co-parent, our economic partner, our emotional support system, our adventure companion. We expect them to meet needs that entire villages once shared. And we do this with no compassion when they fall short, no forgiveness when they fail to be everything we need.

To be everything that someone needs is like playing God. It can be close, but it is hardly ever possible, and the expectation itself can drain a relationship of its joy. Whether it is a parent and child, siblings, or a couple, giving room to be wrong, to fail, to have some space, can be the thread that weaves a beautiful story. Love that lasts makes room for humanity.

The Couple Who Chose Peace Over Perfection

I once knew a couple everyone called "picture perfect." Their photos were flawless, carefully composed and beautifully lit. Their captions were poetic, little windows into what appeared to be an enviable love story. People in their comment sections expressed longing for what they seemed to have.

But behind closed doors, they were exhausted. They were performing a love they had not actually built. They were so focused on appearing happy that they had neglected the work of being happy. The energy that should have gone into their relationship went instead into documenting it, curating it, presenting it for public consumption.

They were in love with the idea of being admired. The validation fed something in both of them, something hungry and unexamined. And for a while, the performance sustained them. But performance is exhausting. Eventually, the gap between the image and the reality became too painful to ignore.

One day, the wife said simply, "I'm tired of pretending." And with those words, everything began to change.

They started therapy. Not because they were broken, but because they wanted to build something real on the foundation that had been neglected. They began to talk honestly about fears, insecurities, triggers, childhood wounds. All the things they had been hiding behind carefully filtered photos and poetic captions.

They started walking instead of posing. Taking actual walks together, where they talked about real things, where they were present with each other rather than performing for an audience. They started praying instead of posting, investing their energy in their actual connection rather than its documentation.

And they started sowing a seed of friendship between them, cultivating a bond that would sustain them when romance left the room. Because romance always leaves the room sometimes. The question is what remains when it does.

Years later, they are still together. Not perfect, but peaceful. Not performing, but present. Their social media is quieter now. Their life is fuller. Because they learned what most never do: Romance does not keep love alive. Truth and friendship do. The pretty parts come and go. The real parts are what remain.

The Bliss of Self-Alignment

When you return home to yourself, when you stop abandoning your own center to chase validation elsewhere, you become magnetic. Not in the manipulative sense, not through technique or strategy, but through authenticity. There is something irresistible about a woman who is at home in her own skin.

You laugh easily, not to perform amusement, but because joy has become accessible to you. You sleep deeply, not because your circumstances are perfect, but because your conscience is clear and your spirit is at rest. You speak gently and confidently, no longer feeling the need to raise your voice to be heard, trusting that your words have weight without aggression.

You are not trying to be loved. You are love. You are not seeking validation. You are generating it from within. You are not performing worthiness. You are living from it.

And when you meet or live with a man who mirrors that energy, a man who has done his own work and arrived at his own wholeness, you do not fight for control. You flow in co-creation. You do not compete with him, and he does not diminish you. You are not trying to win, and neither is he. You are both trying to build.

Together, you create something sacred. A space where respect, safety, and joy coexist. Where growth is expected and supported. Where both people are seen fully and loved anyway. Where the relationship makes both of you better, not because it completes you, but because it inspires you to keep becoming.

Because alignment is the truest aphrodisiac. Not chemistry, which fades. Not attraction, which fluctuates. But alignment, the deep resonance of two souls walking in the same direction, honoring the same values, building toward the same vision. That is what sustains.

Real Love Is Not Transactional

There is a thin line between healthy standards and materialistic illusions. The culture has confused these two things, and many women find themselves caught between them, unsure which one they are actually pursuing.

Wanting stability is wisdom. Wanting a partner who has vision, who knows where he is going and is actively moving in that direction, that is discernment. Wanting emotional maturity, the ability to communicate, to handle conflict well, to show up consistently, that is healthy. These are not shallow desires. They are foundational to partnership.

But demanding perfection from someone human is ego. Creating checklists that no real person could satisfy is not having high standards. It is building walls. It is creating conditions that guarantee disappointment, that ensure you will always find fault, that protect you from the vulnerability of actually receiving love.

We have been misled by gurus who sell "high-value dating" but forget that value has nothing to do with income. Value is about integrity. Value is about how someone treats people who can do nothing for them. Value is about character, the part that remains when no one is watching, when there is no benefit to being good.

A man's car will not make you feel safe if his character does not. You can ride in luxury and still feel alone, still feel unseen, still feel like you are performing for someone who does not truly know you. Material provision without emotional presence is just another form of emptiness.

A woman's beauty will not make her a healthy partner if her peace is performative. If she has not done her own work, if she is projecting wholeness while harboring wounds, if she is presenting calm while chaos churns beneath the surface. Beauty attracts, but it does not sustain. Character sustains.

The world has confused aesthetics with alignment. It has taught us to prioritize what looks good over what is good. But love that lasts is never for sale. It is built. Brick by brick. Choice by choice. Day by day. It is earned not through performance but through presence. Not through appearance but through authenticity.

"Romance makes it pretty. Truth makes it last."

Spiritual Truth

"Let love be genuine. Hate what is evil; cling to what is good." (Romans 12:9)

True love does not hide behind filters or validation. It does not need the approval of strangers to believe in itself. It is not about grand gestures performed for audiences. It is about grace in daily choices, in the small moments that no one sees, in the ordinary Tuesday evenings that will never be photographed.

There is no harm in grand gestures. A surprise trip, a thoughtful gift, a public declaration of affection. These things are beautiful when they come from a place of truth, when they are overflow rather than performance, when they express something real rather than create an appearance.

To love better is to live truthfully. Even when it is quiet. Even when no one is watching. Even when it would be easier to pretend. Love that lasts is built on truth, sustained by truth, purified by truth. It is the foundation that holds when everything else shakes.

Hard Truths

Peaceful love will not give you constant adrenaline. It will not keep you on edge, guessing, anxious. But it will give you rest. The kind of rest that allows you to flourish, to grow, to become more yourself rather than less.

Alignment feels like calm, not confusion. If you are constantly confused, constantly trying to decode signals, constantly uncertain where you stand, that is information. Alignment brings clarity. It feels like coming home.

The most "romantic" thing you can do is tell the truth consistently. Not grand gestures that dazzle then disappear. But steady, reliable honesty. Day after day. Year after year. The willingness to be known and to know.

Love does not prove. It preserves. It does not exhaust itself demonstrating. It quietly sustains. It does not need to be convincing. It simply is, and in being, it endures.

Journal Prompts

Where have I mistaken performance for connection? What was I hoping the performance would earn me?

What does love feel like when I am at peace with myself? How is it different from love I have pursued from a place of insecurity?

How do I show gratitude for the quiet love in my life? Do I value it as much as I value dramatic displays?

What does "choosing myself" look like in my daily life right now? What small choice could I make today to practice this?

Affirmation

I am the love I have been waiting for. I attract truth, peace, and partnership rooted in purpose. I honor love that whispers instead of shouts. I am whole, and from my wholeness, I welcome connections that celebrates rather than completes me.

Closing Truth

You do not have to chase what is aligned with your soul. It recognizes you. It sees you across crowded rooms and busy lives. It mirrors your growth, having done its own growing. It meets you where you have evolved, because it has been evolving too.

Love is not a highlight reel to be curated and presented. It is a healing field where two people tend to what grows between them. Where wounds can be shown without shame. Where growth can happen at its own pace. Where truth is the only acceptable currency.

And when you learn to love yourself fully, completely, without condition, the love that finds you will not need proof. It will not require documentation or validation or performance. It will simply fit. Because what is built on truth does not need performance. It just needs presence. It just needs peace. It just needs two whole people choosing each other, day after day, with clarity and intention.

You are the love you have been waiting for. Start there. Everything else follows.

~

Now that we understand self-love as our foundation, let us explore what makes that love flourish: the power of emotional safety.

CHAPTER FIVE

The Love That Was Good but Not Enough

"Sometimes the hardest goodbye is to the love that almost fit."

There is a man I have loved deeply. Not loudly, not chaotically, but with reverence. We laughed easily, agreed and disagreed respectfully, worked well together in life and business, even in service through nonprofit work. We traveled well, and conversations stretched late into the night. We communicated with respect, apologized without pride, listened, and acknowledged each other's humanity. Just like it should be.

To the outside world, we looked like what everyone hoped for. Even to me, it felt like my prayers for an aligned life partner and family had finally been answered. He embodied kindness, compassion, accountability, and responsibility. Hardworking. God-loving. A devoted father, gentle with me indoors and out, protective when life broke me open. He stood firmly beside me in grief and showed up with strength and tenderness. I thought: *This is it. Surely this is what love looks like.*

And yet, behind closed doors, something essential was missing.

The Love That Confuses You

There is a particular kind of heartbreak that does not come from chaos or cruelty. It comes from love that feels safe, gentle, and almost right. The conversations are kind. The connection feels genuine. There is respect, laughter, shared values, and moments where you think *this could work.* And yet something in your body stays alert. Something never fully lands.

Not because love was absent, but because safety was inconsistent. This is the kind of love that confuses you. where nothing is technically wrong, yet something inside you never fully settles. For a long time, I wondered why it didn't feel like I was enough, until I realized it was not a lack in him, but an invitation for deeper honesty in me. The discomfort was a mirror, quietly asking me to listen beyond my desire and lean into truth. Because when alignment is real, you don't have to abandon yourself to find it. And if the connection had been whole, I would not have been called back to myself with such urgency. Choosing myself became the clearest message love could give me and the lesson I could no longer ignore. I learned I can love someone, miss them and even smile when I had a happy thought about them; and still chose myself, without chaos or drama.

I love how happy and safe I felt around him. When we were together, something in me softened. The little girl in me came out: playful, laughing, unguarded. For the first time in a long time, I felt free to be myself without inhibition, without performance, without armor. That felt rare. That felt sacred. That felt like home.

Around him, the need to impress dissolved. I did not feel like I had to earn affection. I could simply exist, and that alone felt like a miracle. I remember thinking, *How could this not be forever?*

Safety had been something I longed for. And here it was, in moments, in laughter, in what I had accepted as presence.

But love is not only how you feel in the moments that feel good. Love is how something holds you when the moments are uncertain.

The Turning Point

The intimacy I needed never arrived. Not consistently. Not fully.

What confused me most was that there was no villain or cruelty to point to. No disrespect. No chaos. No betrayal. Just a quiet absence where more intimacy should have lived. He showed up when life was heavy but disappeared when love required presence.

I learned to listen with truth instead of desire. To hear what was, not what I wanted to hear. To notice what felt missing without rushing to fill the space with hope or fantasy.

The last time we were physically close was also the first time I truly understood: his avoidance was not rejection. It was not that he did not care. It was a wound he did not know existed or know how to heal yet.

That is when the grief changed. I was not just sad about losing him. I was sad because I realized that although I still loved him, I would never get what I needed if I stayed, and he had done nothing wrong. That required a different kind of courage. Especially when your family and friends see one thing, but what you know is hard to explain. Especially with the fear of starting all over, or looking like a failure.

One day I realized I was not asking for too much. I was asking the wrong person or wrong timing.

My Part in the Pattern

There is something else I must name. Not with shame, but with honesty. I did not cause the distance in that relationship, but I did contribute to the dynamic in ways I could not see at the time.

I chased clarity instead of allowing it to unfold naturally. I gave love where it had not been asked for, hoping it would create safety. I was trying to earn what I already had and ignorant of the value I was already given. I offered reassurance before learning how to sit with my own discomfort.

Not because I was manipulative or malicious, but because I was anxious, unfamiliar with the kind of stillness that kind moment required, and afraid that pausing meant losing.

I did not always allow myself the space to observe, to feel, to process. I rushed to soothe the connection instead of listening to my inner signals, and in doing so, I sometimes crossed my own boundaries, then quietly resented the very thing I had volunteered. That was not toxic. It was ignorance born from long periods of survival.

At the time, I believed love meant effort: giving and anticipating needs before they were spoken. I thought responsiveness equaled devotion and silence meant danger.

Now I know better. Love does not require me to perform emotional labor in advance. It does not ask me to abandon my nervous system to secure closeness. It does not punish me for slowing down and paying attention to myself.

If I could speak to that version of me, I would not scold her. I would thank her for loving deeply with the tools she had, and then I would gently teach her new ones. Especially the fact that not all good relationships have to end forever. Some really amazing ones, can be short lived and it's ok to bless what it was and prepare for the next without tension or resentment.

Today, accountability for me means: I no longer chase clarity. I observe consistency. I no longer give to be chosen. I give when invited. I no longer rush intimacy. I regulate first. I no longer override my intuition to preserve connection. I let love meet me where I stand, not where I bend.

Growth is not pretending we did nothing wrong. It is owning what we did not know and choosing differently once we do.

The Women Who Find Themselves Here

So many women find themselves here. With a man who is kind, admired, and good on paper. With a relationship that looks beautiful to others. With chemistry, shared history, and mutual respect.

And yet you feel alone inside the connection.

You wait. You explain. You hope. You wonder if you are asking for too much.

You are not.

You are asking for alignment, not perfection.

This was the part that hurt the most: the realization that love could feel good and still not be enough. That chemistry could coexist with incompatibility. That comfort could exist alongside misalignment.

I had to choose the person who would be there for me the most, and that person was me.

What Avoidance Can Look Like

From a compassionate perspective, he may have loved me the only way he knew how. Those with avoidant patterns often equate love with duty, protection, and presence in crisis, but feel overwhelmed by sustained intimacy, vulnerability, and emotional dependence.

He may have felt conflicted because he wanted to provide but did not know how to step into that role with someone who did not need saving. And I can hold compassion for that without sacrificing myself to accommodate it.

Understanding a man's wounds does not require a woman to live inside them.

Cultural Roots of Endurance

I was raised in a culture where love was rooted in duty. Where marriage was expected, not explored. Where romance was observed on television, not practiced in real life. My parents were not raised with public displays of affection, wedding bands, white gowns, or French kisses. We saw all that on

TV and tried to fit in with a culture that was not aligned with our own.

Patriarchy also ruled the system, so what many women saw as love and leadership was from a male perspective, and many, not all, tried to mirror that. We were taught to believe that endurance equals virtue.

I had to unlearn the belief that endurance equals virtue. And learn that choosing myself is not selfish. It is sacred. I can love, learn, and lead as a woman with balance and self-love.

No one taught us how to love ourselves. Yet we were expected to know how to give love, receive love, and sustain it flawlessly.

Spiritual Truth

"Above all else, guard your heart, for everything you do flows from it."
(Proverbs 4:23)

I used to think God abandoned me when that relationship did not become what I hoped. But I realized God did not abandon me. By not fixing it, God trusted me enough to let me choose. The gift of free will is also the gift of discernment, of learning to recognize what is for you and what is not.

That understanding helped me hold compassion and love for him without returning to the pattern. I was no longer asking, "Why am I not enough?" I was finally saying, "I need balance, and that is okay."

HARD TRUTHS

Compatibility is not the same as capacity. Someone can share your values, your faith, your vision, and still not have the emotional bandwidth to meet you in partnership.

Respect is not the same as emotional availability. A man can honor you deeply and still be unable to show up for the sustained intimacy a relationship requires.

Shared values do not guarantee shared readiness, even if you both believe in God.

And love alone does not make a partnership sustainable.

You do not need a villain to justify leaving. Sometimes choosing yourself does not come with drama. It comes quietly, with grief and clarity, and with the courage to stop hoping for more from someone who simply does not have it to give.

I stopped asking, "Why isn't this working?" and started asking, "What is this teaching me?"

Love anticipates needs. When Love that is wholesome showed up, I learned that when a man is in love with a woman, her needs and wants become his goals and he gains her respect. Together they can find peace even in chaos. You will never give your new born baby you love so much to someone you don't trust will love them well. Same as you will not abandon yourself to someone who will not value you if you love yourself well. You can only do that when you finally come home to you.

Have you ever felt strong everywhere except in your heart? We tend to be strong for others, for our jobs, for culture, religion, tradition and most of us women tend to be strong for men and not for ourselves. Instead we learn survival, performance and when we don't love ourselves well enough. However, when we learn to love ourselves better, we protect our hearts and make sure it is safe.

I did not imagine the love we had. I did not exaggerate the loss. I did not fail the relationship. I cherished what we shared and graduated from confusing hope with alignment and endurance with devotion.

JOURNAL PROMPTS

Where have I stayed because love was present, even though alignment was not?

What does partnership mean to me now, not based on hope, but on lived truth?

What would it look like to choose myself without resentment or fear?

Where have I given more than was asked of me in order to feel secure?

Affirmation

I honor love that honors me. I choose alignment over attachment. I trust myself to walk away from what cannot meet me fully. I let love meet me where I stand, not where I bend. And that is how I now choose to love myself, even better than I did before.

Closing Truth

I did not lose love. I outgrew a version of it. I did not fail. I chose myself. And that quiet, painful, necessary choice became the doorway to a deeper kind of freedom.

Choosing myself did not erase the tenderness. It did not invalidate the joy, the laughter, or the sense of safety I felt with him. It simply meant I was no longer willing to trade long-term emotional presence for short-term connection.

Sometimes love is not a dramatic rupture. Sometimes it is a quiet knowing. A sacred pause. A choice made in stillness.

And this time, I chose the woman who would never leave me.

Loving him was real. Choosing myself was necessary. And learning the difference changed everything, because the main missing pieces were clarity in commitment, and there is no relationship or partnership without that.

Old habits do not disappear just because closure arrived. They fade slowly, with clarity, with new structure, with consistency and support. But they do fade. And in their place, something stronger grows.

~

Now that we understand that love can be real and still not enough, let us explore what happens when we finally learn to receive the love we deserve.

CHAPTER SIX

The Power of Emotional Safety

"You cannot feel loved where you do not feel safe."

Love feels different when peace walks in. It is quieter than what you knew before, softer than what you were taught to expect. It is more grounded, more rooted, less like a storm and more like the earth itself. It does not make your stomach flip with anxiety masquerading as excitement. It lets your body finally exhale, finally release the breath you did not even know you were holding.

For so many of us, love once meant adrenaline. It meant the rush of uncertainty, the high of not knowing where you stood, the intensity of emotions that swung wildly between ecstasy and despair. We called that love because we did not know any different. We called it passion because chaos was the only language we had learned.

Now, love means ease. It means waking up without dread in your stomach. It means going to sleep without rehearsing arguments in your head. It means trusting that the person beside you will still be there tomorrow, not because they have promised it in heated moments, but because they have proven it through a thousand ordinary choices.

But that ease can be terrifying when all you have ever known is the height of heartbreak. When your nervous system has been calibrated for chaos, peace feels foreign. Unfamiliar. Even wrong. Part of you might wait for the other shoe to drop, for the calm to shatter, for the "real" version of this person to finally emerge. That waiting is not intuition. It is conditioning. It is your body expecting what it has always received.

Because emotional safety is not something we stumble into by accident. It is not luck or chance or finding the right person while unprepared. It is something we learn to allow. Something we must develop the capacity to receive. Something we must recognize as valuable before we can truly let it in.

What Emotional Safety Really Means

Emotional safety is not perfection. It is not a relationship without disagreements, disappointments, or difficult conversations. It is not two people who never trigger each other, never hurt each other, never fall short of each other's expectations. That is not safety. That is fantasy.

Emotional safety is presence. It is the sacred knowing that lives beneath the surface of your interactions, the foundation that holds even when things get shaky. It is knowing, in your bones, that certain things are true:

You can express your truth without being punished. You can say what you actually think, feel what you actually feel, need what you actually need, without fear of retaliation. Your honesty will not be used against you. Your vulnerability will not become ammunition.

You can have a bad day without fear of abandonment. You can be less than your best, can struggle, can fail, can show up imperfect, without worrying that this will be the thing that finally drives them away. There is room for your humanity.

You can disagree and still feel connected. Difference of opinion does not threaten the foundation. You can hold different perspectives, have different preferences, see things differently, without it becoming a referendum on the relationship itself.

Emotional safety is not about never having conflict. Conflict is inevitable between two whole people with their own needs, perspectives, and histories. Safety is about knowing that conflict will not destroy you. That you can move through hard conversations and come out the other side still connected, still committed, still choosing each other.

It is about the ability to breathe with someone, even when the air feels tense. To trust that the tension is temporary. To know that repair is possible and both people are committed to it.

And here is something crucial: emotional safety is not something one person provides while the other receives. It is something two healed people create together. It requires both parties to be committed to honesty, to repair, to showing up with integrity even when it would be easier not to. One person cannot create safety alone. It is always co-created.

The Relationship That Taught Me Calm Was Not Complacency

Maya Angelou's poem "Our Grandmothers" contains a line that has stayed with me: "I come as one, but I stand as ten thousand." It speaks to the strength we carry from those who came before us, the accumulated wisdom of generations that lives in our bones. I think of this when I think about what I have learned about love, how the lessons of those who loved imperfectly before me have shaped my understanding of what love can be.

After years of chaotic love, the kind that made me question my sanity, question my worth, question whether I was capable of being loved at all, I met someone who made me feel something new: safe.

He did not raise his voice. Even in disagreement, even in frustration, his tone remained steady. At first, I did not know what to do with that. I kept waiting for the explosion that never came, bracing for an impact that was not coming.

He did not disappear. When things got hard, he did not withdraw for days, did not punish me with silence, did not make me chase his presence. He stayed. Not perfectly, but consistently. Present even when presence was uncomfortable.

He did not make me question my worth. He did not deliver criticism wrapped as jokes. He did not compare me to other women. He did not make me feel like I had to compete for his attention or prove I deserved his love.

He made me laugh, the real kind of laughter that starts in your belly and surprises you with its own volume. He listened, not while waiting for his turn to speak, but with genuine curiosity about what I was saying. He saw me, not just the version I presented but the woman underneath the presentation.

We had a deep mutual respect, one built on shared values, open communication, and genuine appreciation for who the other person was. For the first time in a long time, I could rest in someone's presence without performing. I could be tired without being judged. I could be uncertain without being dismissed. I could be myself without editing.

But as beautiful as it was, there was something subtle beneath the peace. A quiet fear that neither of us named at first. A fear of losing ourselves again. Not because of toxicity, not because either of us was behaving badly, but because we were both still learning how to love from a healed place. We had each done our own work, but partnership requires a different kind of work. Being whole alone is different from staying whole together.

Sometimes I would catch myself waiting for the chaos that never came. My nervous system scanning for threats that did not exist. He would go silent sometimes to protect his peace, to process, to think before speaking, and I would read it as distance. As withdrawal. As the beginning of the end. We were not fighting. We were adjusting. Learning each other's languages. Discovering that safety does not mean the absence of effort, just a different kind of effort.

One evening, during a long walk as the sun set in colors neither of us stopped to photograph, I said something I had been holding: "I don't want to lose me again."

He nodded slowly. "Me neither."

That moment was not a breakup. It was a breakthrough. We realized that love was not the test. Alignment was. Could we stay true to ourselves while building something together? Could we honor our individual healing while creating shared safety? Could we grow in the same direction without losing our separate identities?

And we passed that test. Not because we were perfect, but because we kept choosing respect over reaction, truth over tension, peace over panic. We kept showing up even when showing up was hard. We kept communicating even when it would have been easier to assume.

We both learned something sacred that day: Safe love still requires courage. Peace is not passivity. Calm is not complacency. It takes bravery to stay open when your history tells you to close. It takes courage to trust when your past has taught you that trust is dangerous.

What Safe Love Feels Like

At first, safety feels foreign. It feels like something is missing, like the absence of drama is the absence of depth. You keep waiting for the red flag to emerge, for the shift in tone that signals danger, for the heartbreak that has always followed connection.

But one day, you realize the calm is not fake. It is not the calm before a storm. It is just calm. You have simply outgrown the chaos that used to excite you. Your nervous system has learned a new baseline. What once felt boring now feels beautiful.

Safe love feels like being able to exhale mid-sentence, knowing you will be heard, knowing you will not be interrupted or dismissed or corrected before you finish your thought.

Safe love feels like having disagreements without emotional warfare, without raised voices or slammed doors, without anyone threatening to leave, without punishment disguised as silence.

Safe love feels like being seen rather than scrutinized, like someone is curious about you rather than evaluating you, like their attention is a gift rather than an inspection.

Safe love feels like being met with compassion instead of criticism, like your struggles are met with support rather than judgment, like your imperfections are held gently rather than weaponized.

Safe love feels like knowing you can be vulnerable and still be valued, that showing your soft places will not make someone lose respect for you, that your tears will not be used as evidence of weakness.

It is love that does not demand your silence to keep the peace. Love that does not require you to shrink, to quiet yourself, to become smaller to maintain harmony. Instead, it invites your truth to build peace. It welcomes your voice as essential to what you are creating together.

When Healing Meets Love

When two people meet after healing, when both have done the work of understanding their patterns and tending to their wounds, the relationship feels like both a mirror and a magnifier. You see your progress reflected back to you, all the ways you have grown, all the old patterns you no longer repeat. And you also see your triggers, amplified by intimacy, rising to the surface in ways they could not when you were alone.

You feel your peace and your edges. The calm you have cultivated and the places where that calm still wavers. The confidence you have built and the insecurities that still whisper in quiet moments. Partnership has a way of revealing what solitude could conceal.

But unlike before, you do not run. You do not flee at the first sign of difficulty, convinced that discomfort means you are with the wrong person. You do not accuse, projecting your fears onto them, making them responsible for wounds they did not create. You communicate. You pause. You pray. You grow together, not against each other.

You learn that fear can coexist with love. This is perhaps the most important lesson. Fear does not have to be eliminated to move forward. It just does not have to drive the car anymore. It can sit in the backseat. It can be acknowledged without being obeyed. You can feel afraid and still choose trust. You can feel uncertain and still choose to stay.

Somatic Practices for Creating Internal Safety

Emotional safety is not only created through conversations and commitments. It is built in the body. Your nervous system needs to learn, through repeated experience, that safety is possible. Here are practices that can help you create internal safety, regardless of your external circumstances:

Grounding Through the Senses: When you feel triggered or anxious, bring yourself into the present moment by engaging your five senses. Name five things you can see. Four things you can touch. Three things you can hear. Two things you can smell. One thing you can taste. This practice interrupts the spiral of anxious thoughts and anchors you in the present, where you are actually safe.

The 4-7-8 Breath: This breathing technique activates your parasympathetic nervous system, the part responsible for rest and calm. Inhale through your nose for four counts. Hold your breath for seven counts. Exhale slowly through your mouth for eight counts. Repeat this cycle four times. Practice it daily, not just when you are anxious, so your body learns this rhythm as a pathway to peace.

The Self-Hold: When you feel activated, place one hand on your heart and one on your belly. Apply gentle pressure. Feel the warmth of your own touch. This simple gesture activates the same neural pathways that are activated when someone else holds you. Breathe slowly and speak to yourself as you would to a frightened child: "You are safe. You are okay. This feeling will pass."

The Body Scan: Before difficult conversations or when you notice tension building, take a moment to scan your body from head to toe. Notice where you are holding tension. Consciously relax those areas. Unclench your jaw. Drop your shoulders. Soften your belly. Release your hands. Bringing awareness to physical tension allows you to release it before it influences your words and reactions.

These practices are not one-time fixes. They are daily investments in your capacity for safety. The more you practice when you are calm, the more accessible they become when you are activated. You are literally building new neural pathways, teaching your body that there is another way to respond.

Learning to Receive What Was Offered

A friend once told me she used to sabotage every good relationship. Whenever things got too peaceful, she would pick fights over nothing, create drama where none existed, or pull away without explanation. She said, "I didn't know how to exist without chaos. Peace felt like the calm before a storm, and I figured I might as well get the storm started on my own terms."

Her pattern made sense when you understood her history. She had grown up in a home where tension was constant, where good moments were always followed by explosions, where waiting for the other shoe to drop was the safest strategy because the shoe always dropped. Her nervous system had learned that vigilance was survival. That peace was just the setup for pain.

So when she met someone emotionally grounded, someone who did not create chaos, who did not play games, who showed up consistently and communicated clearly, her system did not know what to do. The absence of drama felt like a threat. The presence of stability felt unstable.

But this time, she decided to do something new. Instead of reacting from her old patterns, she reflected. She got curious about her own responses instead of acting on them automatically.

When he was quiet, she breathed instead of spiraling. She reminded herself that his silence might mean he was processing, not withdrawing. That his need for space was not a precursor to leaving.

When she was triggered, she communicated instead of testing him. Instead of creating situations to see if he would stay, she told him directly what she was feeling, what she was afraid of, what she needed.

She said something that stayed with me: "I realized emotional safety wasn't something he had to prove. It was something I had to receive." He was already offering it. She just had to learn to let it in, to believe it was real, to trust that it would last.

The Nervous System of Love

Our bodies remember what the mind forgets. This is both a blessing and a burden. It means we carry wisdom in our cells, intuition in our gut, knowledge that does not require conscious thought. But it also means we carry wounds, automatic responses, patterns laid down before we had words to describe them.

That is why healing is not only emotional or spiritual. It is biological. It lives in the body. Your nervous system has its own memory, its own expectations, its own predictions about what will happen next based on what has happened before. And those predictions influence everything: who you are attracted to, how you interpret behavior, what feels like love and what feels like danger.

Every time you choose calm over chaos, you are rewiring your nervous system. You are teaching it that peace is not dangerous, that safety is not a trap, that good things can last.

Every time you stay instead of self-sabotaging, you are expanding your capacity for intimacy. You are proving to your body that connection does not have to end in pain, that vulnerability does not always lead to betrayal.

Every time you communicate instead of shutting down, you are teaching your body that love can be safe. That your voice matters. That expressing your needs does not result in abandonment.

This is why emotional safety is a practice, not a promise. It is not something you achieve once and possess forever. It is something you build through consistent truth, through time invested, through tenderness offered and received. It requires daily attention, daily choice, daily commitment to showing up in ways that reinforce safety rather than undermine it.

The Paradox of Safety

Emotional safety does not mean you will never be triggered. It does not mean you will glide through your relationship without ever feeling activated, defensive, or afraid. That is not realistic, not for two humans with histories and wounds and nervous systems that remember.

What it means is that when you are triggered, both of you know how to hold space for it. Both of you understand that activation is information, not accusation. Both of you can recognize when the past is intruding on the present and can navigate that intrusion together.

Safety is not a guarantee against pain. It is a commitment to repair. A promise that when hurt happens, as it inevitably will between two imperfect people, you will turn toward each other rather than away. You will address it rather than bury it. You will heal it rather than let it fester.

You learn to say things that once felt impossible:

"I need a moment." Not as a punishment or a withdrawal, but as a recognition that you need to regulate before you can communicate effectively.

"I feel misunderstood. Can we talk about it?" An invitation rather than an accusation. A request for clarity rather than a demand for vindication.

"I love you, and I also need space." Both things are true at once. Love and need for distance not contradictory but coexisting.

Because real intimacy is not about constant closeness. It is about emotional honesty. It is about being able to name what is happening inside you and trust that the naming will be received with care.

Spiritual Reflection

When I think about safety, I think about how Jesus loved. Never through manipulation or fear. Never through control or coercion. But through presence and understanding. Through patience and grace.

He never forced love. He invited it. He offered Himself and allowed people to respond freely. He did not manipulate emotions to create attachment. He simply was who He was and let that be enough.

He never demanded perfection. He offered grace. He met people where they were, in their mess, in their failure, in their doubt. He did not require them to clean themselves up before approaching. He welcomed them as they were and loved them toward who they could become.

"There is no fear in love. But perfect love drives out fear." (1 John 4:18)

When love is rooted in truth, fear loses its grip. Not immediately, not completely, but progressively. Each experience of being loved without condition, being met with grace instead of judgment, chips away at the fear that once seemed immovable.

When both people are healed enough to stay honest, when both are committed to truth even when it is uncomfortable, safety becomes the soil where intimacy grows. Not perfect safety. Not the absence of all risk. But the presence of commitment to truth, to repair, to love that does not abandon when things get hard.

Hard Truths

Emotional safety is not built through passion. It is built through patience. The slow, daily work of showing up. The unglamorous consistency that no one posts about but everyone needs.

The person who truly loves you will prioritize peace, not prove it. They will not perform safety for an audience. They will simply create it, quietly, consistently, in the thousand small moments that make up a life together.

Love is not about avoiding triggers. That is not possible between two humans with histories. It is about holding hands through them. About staying present when activation happens. About being a safe place for each other's wounds to surface and heal.

If you still have to perform to feel safe, you are not healed. You are hiding. True safety does not require performance. It receives authenticity. If you are still editing yourself, still shrinking, still becoming someone you are not in order to maintain the relationship, that is not safety. That is survival wearing safety's clothes.

"Real love doesn't make you guess. It makes you grow."

Journal Prompts

What does emotional safety feel like in my body? Where do I feel it? What sensations tell me I am safe?

How do I react when I feel misunderstood, and what would a safe version of me do instead? What old pattern gets activated?

Who in my life has made me feel emotionally safe, and what did they do differently? What can I learn from that experience?

Which somatic practice (grounding, breathing, self-hold, body scan) resonates most with me? When could I practice it this week?

Affirmation

I am safe within myself. I build love that honors truth, calm, and communication. I choose connection over control, peace over panic, and grace over fear. I am worthy of love that does not require my performance, only my presence.

Closing Truth

Emotional safety does not make love boring. It makes it sustainable. It provides the foundation that allows everything else to flourish. Without safety, there is no true intimacy, only performance. Without safety, there is no real vulnerability, only the appearance of it.

Safety is the quiet rhythm of peace after the noise of proving. It is the moment you realize that love is not meant to test your worth. It is meant to witness it. To see you, really see you, and choose to stay.

And when two people commit to protecting peace more than performing passion, when they value the daily work of trust-building over the occasional drama of intensity, that is when love becomes a sanctuary. Not a struggle. Not a storm to be weathered. But a place of rest. A place of becoming. A place where both people can finally exhale.

You deserve that. A sanctuary, not a struggle. A safe place to land.

~

Now that we understand the power of emotional safety, let us explore how to rebuild trust with the one person whose trust matters most: yourself.

CHAPTER SEVEN

Self-Trust and the Woman Within

"When you stop betraying yourself, the world starts to respond differently."

Opening Scene

There comes a time when the loudest voice in the room is no longer outside of you. No longer the opinions of others, the expectations of society, the criticism of those who do not understand your journey. The loudest voice becomes the whisper within, the one that rises from somewhere deeper than thought, the one that says simply, quietly, with unshakeable certainty: "You already know."

You begin to realize that intuition is not a mystery. It is not some mystical gift given to a special few. It is memory. Your soul remembering what truth feels like. Your body recognizing patterns it has seen before, even when your conscious mind has not caught up. Your spirit confirming what alignment actually is, what it feels like when something is right for you and what it feels like when something is wrong.

Self-trust is the bridge between who you were and who you are becoming. It is the structure that allows you to cross from the woman who needed everyone's approval to the woman who only needs her own. It is how you stop abandoning yourself to be accepted by others. It is how you stop betraying your own knowing to maintain relationships that require your silence. It is how you return home to your own voice, the one that was always there, waiting beneath the noise for you to finally listen.

This chapter is about that return. About rebuilding the relationship with the most important person in your life: yourself. About learning to trust the woman within who has been guiding you all along, even when you did not realize she was speaking.

The Cost of Self-Betrayal

For years, I mistook compliance for kindness. I thought being agreeable was the same as being good. I thought saying yes to everything made me generous, accommodating, easy to love. I did not realize I was slowly erasing myself, one agreement at a time.

I said "yes" when my soul screamed "no." I felt the resistance in my body, the tightening in my stomach, the heaviness in my chest, but I overrode it. I told myself I was being flexible. I was being a team player. I was being mature enough to set aside my own preferences for the good of others. But the truth was simpler and sadder: I was afraid. Afraid of conflict. Afraid of disappointment. Afraid that my real answer would cost me love.

I over-explained, offering reasons and justifications for things that needed no explanation. I overgave, pouring myself out until I was empty, then pouring some more. I overstayed in situations that had long stopped serving me, convinced that leaving would be failure, that persistence was the same as commitment, that my discomfort was a price worth paying for belonging.

I thought that was what love demanded. Complete surrender. Total accommodation. The erasure of my own needs in service of someone else's comfort.

But every time I silenced myself to keep the peace, I was teaching my nervous system something dangerous. I was teaching it that my truth was a threat. That my voice was a problem to be managed. That the safest thing I could do was disappear, become smaller, become quieter, become whatever was required to avoid the discomfort of being myself.

And nothing drains the spirit faster than constantly betraying what you know is right. The exhaustion is not physical, though it manifests there eventually. It is soul-deep. It is the fatigue of living in constant contradiction, of saying one thing while feeling another, of smiling while screaming inside.

Self-betrayal is subtle. It does not announce itself with dramatic gestures. It whispers. It rationalizes. It sounds reasonable, even wise.

It sounds like: "Maybe I'm overreacting." A dismissal of your own experience. A suggestion that your feelings are too big, too sensitive, too much. But your feelings are information. They are data about your inner state. Dismissing them as overreaction is dismissing yourself.

It sounds like: "He didn't mean it like that." A reinterpretation of someone else's behavior to make it more acceptable, to avoid the discomfort of acknowledging what you actually experienced. But you know what you experienced. Rewriting it to protect someone else is betraying yourself.

It sounds like: "If I just try harder, it'll get better." The belief that your effort is the variable, that if things are not working, it must be because you have not given enough. But sometimes things are not working because they were never meant to work. Sometimes the answer is not more effort but honest acknowledgment.

Every small betrayal compounds. They accumulate like interest on a debt, growing heavier with each repetition. Until one day your inner voice stops speaking. Not because she is gone. She is never gone. But because she is tired of being ignored. She has learned that you will not listen, so she has stopped wasting her breath. The silence is not peace. It is resignation.

Learning to Listen Again

A few years ago, I found myself at yet another crossroads. The kind of decision point that feels both mundane and monumental, ordinary on the surface but potentially life-altering beneath.

A business partnership had presented itself. It looked promising by every external measure. The numbers were right. The opportunities seemed endless. The other party was well-connected, experienced, successful in ways I aspired to be. On paper, it was exactly what I had been praying for.

But my body felt tight every time I got on a call. My chest would constrict. My breath would be shallow. I would hang up feeling drained rather than energized, unsettled rather than excited. Something was off, but I could not name it. There was nothing objectively wrong. No red flags I could point to. Just a persistent discomfort that would not be released.

For weeks I rationalized it away. I told myself I was just afraid of success. That this was imposter syndrome showing up to sabotage a good thing. That my discomfort was a sign I was growing, stepping outside my comfort zone, becoming the woman who could handle bigger opportunities.

I almost convinced myself. Almost.

Until one morning, in prayer, in that quiet space where my defenses were down and my rationalizations could not reach, I heard it clearly. Not an audible voice, but a knowing that rose from somewhere deeper than thought. "This isn't alignment. It's an attachment."

I was attached to the idea of what this partnership could bring. Attached to the validation of being chosen by someone successful. Attached to the external markers that would prove I was making it. But I was not aligned with the reality of what it actually was, with what my body was trying to tell me every time we spoke.

I ended the partnership. It was not easy. There were awkward conversations and disappointed expectations. Part of me wondered if I was making a mistake, if I would look back on this moment with regret.

But the relief was instant. Not because I had won something, but because I had listened. I had honored my own knowing even when it could not be logically defended. I had trusted myself even when trust felt risky.

That single act of obedience to my own intuition built more confidence than any applause ever could.

More than any external validation. More than any success achieved by ignoring my inner voice. Because when you trust yourself, peace becomes your reward. Not an achievement. Not approval. Peace.

The Re-Parenting of You

Every woman carries a younger version of herself inside. She is still there, that little girl, preserved in the amber of memory. She remembers the first time she was dismissed, her concerns waved away as unimportant. She remembers the first time her truth was too loud, when she was told to be quiet, to be polite, to stop making so much noise. She remembers the first time her softness was punished, when being tender was treated as weakness, when she learned to harden herself to survive.

She carries those moments with her, even now. They shaped how she moves through the world, how she protects herself, what she believes she deserves. The adult woman you have become was built on the foundation of what that little girl learned. And some of what she learned no longer serves you.

Self-trust is how you re-parent her. It is how you become the adult she needed but did not have. The one who listens when she speaks. The one who takes her concerns seriously. The one who protects her from harm without requiring her to harden.

You do not silence her anymore. You do not tell her she is overreacting. You do not dismiss her fears as irrational. You soothe her. You acknowledge what she feels. You say, "I see you. I hear you. I have got us now."

This is not a metaphor. This is practice. When you feel that old fear rising, when you find yourself slipping into patterns that do not serve you, pause. Ask yourself: "How old do I feel right now?" Often, you will find that you are responding from a much younger place than your actual age. The scared child has taken the wheel, reacting from old programming.

In those moments, speak to her directly. Not out loud if that feels strange, but internally. Tell her she is safe. Tell her you will protect her. Tell her she does not have to manage this alone anymore because you are here now, grown and capable and committed to her well-being.

When you keep your word to yourself, you are teaching her that it is finally safe to believe you. When you show up when you say you will, she learns that your promises mean something. When you rest when you promise to, she learns that her needs matter. When you speak when you feel afraid, she learns that her voice is valuable, that it will not be punished.

Every kept promise to yourself is a deposit in the account of self-trust. Every time you honor your word to yourself, you are rebuilding the bond that fear and circumstance once fractured. You are becoming someone she can rely on. And that is everything.

What Trust Looks Like in Action

Trust is not built through grand declarations. It is not a single dramatic moment where everything changes. It is built through small, consistent acts of integrity. Through the daily choices that no one else sees but that you know you have made.

Trust looks like saying "no" without apology. Not "no, but let me explain why." Not "no, I'm sorry, I just can't right now." Just "no." A complete sentence. A full response. An acknowledgment that your refusal needs no justification, that your boundary is its own reason.

Trust looks like following through on what you start. The projects you begin, finishing them or consciously deciding to release them. The commitments you make to yourself, honoring them with the same respect you would give to commitments made to others. Treating your word to yourself as binding.

Trust looks like leaving when peace leaves. Recognizing when a space, a conversation, a relationship has stopped serving you and having the courage to exit. Not staying out of guilt or obligation or fear of what leaving might say about you. Trusting that your peace is important enough to protect.

Trust looks like choosing rest instead of rushing. Recognizing when your body is tired and honoring that tiredness instead of pushing through. Understanding that rest is not laziness but wisdom, that your capacity is not unlimited, that caring for yourself is not indulgence but necessity.

Trust looks like letting your intuition lead even when logic hesitates. Honoring the knowing that cannot be explained, the sense that something is right or wrong even when you cannot articulate why. Trusting that you know more than you can prove.

Every time you honor an inner nudge, every time you listen to that quiet voice and act on what it tells you, you repair the bond with yourself that fear once fractured. You prove to yourself that you are trustworthy. That you will listen. That you will act. That you will protect.

The Mirror Moment

A client once told me she had spent most of her life seeking advice before making any decision. It did not matter how small the choice or how clear the answer seemed. She could not trust her own judgment.

"Even when I knew the answer," she said, "I'd still call five people to confirm it. I'd ask my mom, my sister, my best friend, maybe a coworker. I'd gather opinions like evidence, as if the right answer would emerge from consensus."

She traced this pattern back to her childhood, to a home where her opinions were dismissed and her judgment was questioned. She learned early that her own knowing was not to be trusted, that safety came from external validation, that the only reliable answer was someone else's answer.

One day, on a whim, she stood in front of her bathroom mirror. She looked at herself, really looked, and asked out loud: "What do you think?"

And then she answered. Her own voice, speaking her own truth, making her own decision without external input.

She told me later, "It felt strange at first. Like talking to a stranger. I barely recognized the woman in the mirror as someone whose opinion mattered. But after a while, I realized she was the only voice I could truly trust. She was the one who had lived my life, who knew my history, who understood my values. Everyone else was guessing. She was the only one who actually knew."

That is the essence of self-trust. When your reflection stops needing reassurance and starts giving direction. When the woman in the mirror transforms from someone you are trying to figure out into someone you listen to. When you finally understand that the expert on your life has always been you.

Daily Rituals for Building Self-Trust

Self-trust is not built overnight. It is cultivated through daily practice, through rituals that reinforce your commitment to yourself. Here are practices you can implement to strengthen the relationship with your own knowing:

Morning Check-In: Before you check your phone, before you consume anyone else's thoughts or agendas, spend five minutes in silence. Ask yourself: "How am I really feeling today? What does my body need? What does my spirit need?" Listen for the answers without judgment. This practice trains you to consult yourself first, to prioritize your inner voice over external noise.

The Daily Promise: Each morning, make one small promise to yourself and keep it. It can be simple: "I will drink enough water today." "I will take a ten-minute walk." "I will go to bed by ten." The size of the promise matters less than your commitment to keeping it. Each kept promise builds evidence that you are trustworthy.

Intuition Journaling: At the end of each day, write down any moments when you felt an intuitive nudge. Did you follow it? What happened? Over time, you will build a record of your intuition's accuracy. You will see patterns. You will learn to trust what your body has been trying to tell you.

The Pause Practice: Before making decisions, especially ones involving other people's requests, pause. Say, "Let me think about that and get back to you." This simple delay creates space between stimulus and response, allowing your true answer to emerge rather than your automatic, people-pleasing response. Over time, this pause becomes a doorway to your authentic voice.

These rituals are scaffolding. They support the building of something larger: a life where you are your own first consultant, where your inner voice is honored, where self-trust is not occasional but foundational.

When Love Meets a Woman Who Trusts Herself

She becomes magnetic. Not because she is perfect, not because she has eliminated all her flaws, but because she is peaceful. She has settled into herself. She is no longer at war with her own knowing. And that peace radiates outward, drawing others toward her without effort.

She does not chase. She does not pursue people who are not pursuing her, does not try to convince anyone of her value, does not exhaust herself proving she is worthy of attention. Instead, she chooses. She evaluates what is presented to her and makes decisions from clarity rather than desperation.

She does not manipulate. She does not play games to create interest, does not strategize about when to text back or how to appear mysterious. She magnetizes. Her authenticity draws the right people toward her. Her groundedness creates a gravitational pull that does not require effort to maintain.

A man who meets such a woman feels her confidence like calm water. It steadies him. It shows him what it looks like to be at peace with oneself. He is not destabilized by her presence but anchored by it. He knows he is with someone who does not need saving, just respecting. Someone who is not looking for him to complete her but to complement her. Someone who brings her own wholeness to the relationship rather than seeking wholeness through it.

And in that sacred exchange, both people flourish. Not despite her self-trust but because of it. She creates space for him to trust himself too. She models what it looks like being rooted in your own knowing. She demonstrates that strength and softness can coexist.

Because self-trust does not create distance. It creates clarity. It removes the fog of insecurity that clouds connection. It allows both people to see each other clearly, to choose each other intentionally, to build together on a foundation of truth rather than performance.

And clarity, it turns out, is the purest form of intimacy. Knowing and being known. Seeing and being seen. Without the distortion of desperation or the filter of fear.

Spiritual Reflection

God never designed you to live in confusion. He did not create you to wander through life uncertain of your own knowing, dependent on everyone else's opinion to find your way. He placed intuition in you as divine navigation. That inner voice is not random. It is not imagination. It is the Spirit within you, guiding you toward truth.

Every time you second-guess your discernment, you are doubting more than yourself. You are doubting the Spirit that dwells within you. You are questioning whether God equipped you adequately, whether His presence in your life actually produces wisdom you can trust.

"Trust in the Lord with all your heart and lean not on your own understanding." (Proverbs 3:5)

This verse is not a call to distrust yourself. It is an invitation to align your understanding with divine understanding. To recognize that when your spirit and God's Spirit agree, that agreement produces a knowing that transcends logic. Trust is not the absence of uncertainty. It is the presence of alignment. When your spirit and your steps agree, when your inner knowing and your outer actions match, peace follows.

Self-trust and trust in God are not opposites. They are partners. You trust yourself because you trust the God who made you, who dwells within you, who speaks through your intuition when you are quiet enough to hear.

HARD TRUTHS

You cannot hear God clearly if you are committed to ignoring yourself. The same stillness that allows divine voice to reach you is the stillness that amplifies your own inner knowing. If you have trained yourself to dismiss your intuition, you will dismiss the Spirit speaking through it.

Confidence is built, not borrowed. You cannot absorb it from someone else. You cannot purchase it through achievements or acquire it through relationships. It is constructed from the inside out, through kept promises and honored boundaries, through the slow accumulation of evidence that you are trustworthy.

Intuition becomes louder when you stop crowding it with other people's opinions. The more voices you consult, the harder it becomes to hear your own. There is wisdom in counsel, yes, but there is also wisdom in silence. In making space for your own knowing to emerge before you bury it under everyone else's.

Boundaries are not walls. They are mirrors reflecting your self-respect. Every boundary you set is a statement about what you believe you deserve. Every boundary you enforce is evidence that you trust yourself enough to protect yourself.

"The woman who trusts her intuition will never compete for attention."

Journal Prompts

> *When have I felt my intuition speak clearly, and did I honor it? What happened as a result?*

What promises have I made to myself that I need to keep? What is one small promise I can make and keep this week?

How can I show my younger self that I am safe to trust again? What does she need to hear from me?

Which daily ritual (morning check-in, daily promise, intuition journaling, pause practice) could I implement starting today?

Affirmation

I honor my inner knowing. I am loyal to my peace, faithful to my word, and gentle with my growth. I trust myself because I trust the God within me. My intuition is valid. My voice matters. My knowing is enough.

Closing Truth

The woman within you is not waiting for another apology. She has heard enough apologies, enough promises that were not kept, enough "I'll do better" that never translated into action. She is waiting for consistency. For evidence. For proof that this time will be different.

Every time you choose your truth, she exhales. She feels the relief of finally being heard.

Every time you honor your boundaries, she smiles. She feels the safety of being protected.

Every time you pause and listen, she feels safe again. She trusts that you will not abandon her anymore.

Self-trust is not arrogance. It is not ego or pride or thinking you are better than others. It is an agreement with your Creator. It is saying, "You made me with wisdom and intuition, and I choose to honor what You placed in me." It is stewardship of the knowledge you were given.

And once you trust yourself deeply, once that trust becomes foundational rather than occasional, the world no longer confuses you. Not because it has become simpler, but because your peace has become your compass. You know where you stand. You know what you believe. You know what you deserve.

The woman within is waiting. She has been waiting a long time. But she is patient, because she knows you are worth it. And she believes that one day, you will believe it too.

~

Now that we have rebuilt trust with ourselves, let us explore what it means to bring that whole self into soulful love.

CHAPTER EIGHT

Soulful Love Deserves a Soulful You

"You can't call in peace while still worshipping chaos."

Opening Scene

There is a version of you that does not chase love. She does not pursue it frantically, does not construct elaborate strategies to attract it, does not contort herself into shapes designed to be more appealing. She attracts it simply by how she lives. By the peace that radiates from her presence. By the wholeness that does not require completion from anyone else.

She is not desperate, grasping at any connection that presents itself, so hungry for love that she will accept anything that resembles it. She is not detached, hardened by past pain into someone who cannot receive what is offered, who pushes away what she secretly wants. She is not defensive, armored against vulnerability, unable to let anyone close enough to truly know her.

She is discerning. She knows what she wants and what she will accept. She knows the difference between what feels exciting and what feels aligned. She trusts herself enough to wait for what matches her, rather than forcing herself to match whatever arrives.

She wakes up, pours her tea, and greets the day like a woman who knows her worth. Not arrogantly, not loudly, but quietly and certainly. The knowing lives in her bones, in the way she moves, in the decisions she makes before anyone else is watching.

She is not waiting for someone to text her "good morning" to feel valued. She has already given herself one. She has already spoken kindly to her reflection. She has already acknowledged that this day matters, that she matters, that her existence does not require external validation to be significant.

And that is what makes her magnetic. Not strategy. Not performance. Not the right combination of words and behaviors designed to attract. Just peace. Just wholeness. Just the quiet confidence of a woman who has come home to herself and no longer needs anyone else to tell her she belongs there.

Real love, the kind that lasts, the kind that sustains, the kind worth having, does not come to those who hustle for attention. It does not reward the most persistent pursuit or the cleverest strategy. It comes to those who embody peace. It recognizes its own frequency and moves toward it. It finds the women who have stopped searching frantically and started living fully.

Love Isn't Something You Find: It's Something You Practice

We were raised to believe that love is this grand, cinematic event. The moment when the music swells, when the man appears from across the room, when eyes meet and the world stops spinning. The moment when life suddenly makes sense, when all the waiting and longing and hoping finally pays off in one dramatic revelation.

But real love does not play background music. It builds breakfast routines. It shows up in the mundane moments that no one will ever photograph. It lives in the space between grand gestures, in the ordinary Tuesday mornings and the quiet Sunday evenings and the unremarkable Wednesday afternoons.

Real love is not just candlelit dinners and romantic getaways. It is washing dishes together after a long day. It is laughing at something silly that no one else would understand. It is sitting quietly in the same room, not needing to fill the air with conversation, comfortable enough in each other's presence to simply exist together.

And sometimes, perhaps most importantly, real love is being alone and realizing that your own company feels like safety, not silence. That solitude is not a waiting room for partnership but a complete experience in itself. That you can be happy, genuinely happy, with no one else present. That your wholeness does not depend on another person's presence.

If you cannot enjoy your own presence, you will always make someone else your escape route. Every relationship will carry the weight of your self-abandonment. Every partner will be tasked, consciously or not, with filling a void that is yours to fill. And that is not fair to them, and it is not sustainable for you.

Love is not something you find once and possess forever. It is something you practice daily. In how you treat yourself. In how you show up for others. In how you navigate conflict and celebrate joy. In how you choose, again and again, to be present with what is rather than longing for what is not.

The Everyday Woman's Truth

Let us be honest. Most women do not wake up glowing and meditating with rose quartz, perfectly centered before the day begins. They do not greet the sunrise with yoga poses and green smoothies and gratitude journals filled with elegant handwriting. That is a beautiful image, and for some women it is real, but for most of us, mornings look quite different.

Most women wake up juggling ten tabs in their heads before their feet hit the floor. Bills that need paying. Children that need feeding. Deadlines that are approaching faster than preparation. Relationships that need attention. The search for mascara that has somehow migrated to an unknown location since yesterday. The mental load that no one sees, but that weighs heavily, nonetheless.

We do not need another guru telling us to "raise our vibration." We do not need another Instagram post suggesting that if we just thought positive thoughts hard enough, everything would align. We do not need to feel guilty for not being more enlightened, more centered, more together.

We need to raise our standards for peace. Not perfection, but peace. The kind of peace that can exist alongside imperfection. The kind that does not require everything to be handled before it can be felt. The kind that lives in small moments, stolen from busy days, reclaimed from schedules that leave little room for stillness.

Soulful love starts there. In the quiet, unfiltered moments where you stop pretending to have it all together and simply breathe. In the acceptance of your own humanity. In the permission you give yourself to be a work in progress. In the grace you extend to the woman in the mirror who is doing her best with what she has.

You do not have to have everything figured out to deserve love. You do not have to be fully healed to be worthy of connection. You just have to be honest. With yourself. With others. With the life you are actually living, not the one you perform for audiences.

When She Stopped Trying So Hard

A friend once told me she used to "date like it was a full-time job." She had systems and strategies. She had the right apps and the right photos and the right opening messages. She treated the search for love like a project to be managed, a problem to be solved through sufficient effort and optimization.

Every first date was a mini performance. Full makeup, carefully chosen outfit, mental rehearsals of what she would say and how she would say it. She practiced appearing more relaxed than she felt, more confident than she was, more chill than her racing heart suggested. She was auditioning for a role, and she had studied her lines carefully.

By date three, she would have already built an imaginary future in her mind. The wedding venue. The first apartment together. The inside jokes they would develop. She would invest in this future while simultaneously stressing about whether he would text back, analyzing every message for hidden meanings, interpreting silence as rejection.

Then one day, exhausted from the constant performance, she said something that changed everything: "I just got tired of auditioning for a role I didn't even want anymore."

The role she had been auditioning for was not "partner to someone who truly saw her." It was "an acceptable version of herself that might be chosen." She had been trying so hard to be what she thought men wanted that she had lost touch with who she actually was. And she was exhausted from performing a character she no longer recognized.

So she stopped. Not dating but performing. She went on dates as herself. No masks, no pretense, no emotional makeup covering her real face. She wore what she actually wanted to wear. She said what she actually thought. She did not pretend to like things she did not like or hide opinions she actually held.

And you know what happened? She laughed more. Real laughter, the kind that surprises you, not the polite, performed laughter designed to make someone feel interesting. She ate fries without shame, without worrying about whether eating carbs on a date was attractive. She left when the conversation was dry, not staying out of politeness or hope that things would improve.

And eventually, she met someone who did not fall for her performance, because she was not performing anymore. He fell for her peace. For her authenticity. For the woman who showed up without pretense and trusted that she was enough exactly as she was.

She said something that stayed with me: "I realized I wasn't looking for a man anymore. I was looking for me. And when I found her, he found us both."

Respecting Men Without Losing Yourself

Let us clear something up, because this point gets confused in many conversations about self-love and feminine power: Loving yourself does not mean dismissing men. It does not mean viewing them as obstacles to your wholeness or competitors for power. It does not mean hardening yourself against partnership or rejecting the possibility of genuine connection.

Respecting your feminine essence does not mean rejecting the masculine. The two are not in competition. They are complementary energies, designed to work together, to create something neither can create alone. When we pit them against each other, everyone loses.

There are still good men. They exist, despite what cultural narratives sometimes suggest. Steady men who do not need drama to feel alive. Kind men who lead with compassion rather than control. Protective men who understand that their strength is meant to create safety, not domination. Imperfect men who are nonetheless intentional about growth, about partnership, about becoming better versions of themselves.

These men do not compete with women. They cover them. Not in a diminishing way, not in a way that suggests women are incapable, but in a way that creates shelter. They want to build, not battle. They see partnership as collaboration, not conquest. They understand that a strong woman does not threaten their masculinity but complements it.

And the truth that gets lost in many modern conversations is this: A man feels most seen when he feels respected, just like a woman feels most loved when she feels safe. These are not competing needs. They are complementary ones. When both needs are honored, both people flourish.

The dance between masculine and feminine is not about power. It is not about who leads and who follows, who wins and who loses. It is about partnership. It is about learning to let him lead in his areas of strength without losing your voice, without abandoning your own wisdom, without disappearing into his vision. And it is about him learning to listen without losing his edge, to receive your perspective without feeling diminished, to make space for your strength without feeling threatened by it.

That is balance. That is maturity. That is real love. Not domination or submission, but mutual honoring. Not competition, but collaboration. Two whole people bringing their wholeness together, creating something greater than either could create alone.

The Trap of Artificial Love and Beauty

We live in an age where love has filters. Where feelings are curated for public consumption. Where relationships are documented, edited, and presented as highlight reels. Everyone looks happy on social media. Everyone appears to be living their best life, surrounded by love that looks effortless and beauty that seems natural.

Until you see their eyes in person. Until you sit across from someone whose online presence suggests perfection and realize they are just as lost as anyone else. Just as wounded. Just as uncertain. The filter cannot hide what the eyes reveal.

The truth that no one posts about? No amount of contour can cover emotional neglect. You can look flawless in photographs and feel invisible in your own home. You can present beauty to the world while receiving cruelty behind closed doors.

No luxury vacation can fix loneliness. The most exotic destinations cannot compensate for disconnection. You can stand in paradise and feel utterly alone if the person beside you does not truly see you.

And no "relationship goals" picture can show you the tears, therapy, and truth that real love requires. The image captures a moment. It does not capture the work that made that moment possible, or the pain that preceded it, or the challenges that will follow it.

There is nothing wrong with wanting to look good. Polish your crown. Take care of yourself. Present yourself in ways that make you feel confident and beautiful. But do not let your reflection become a costume. Do not let the external become a substitute for the internal. Do not invest more in appearing loved than in actually being loved.

Because beauty without depth may attract attention. It may gather followers and likes and admiring comments. But only authenticity sustains connection. Only truth builds the kind of intimacy that lasts. Only real, unfiltered presence creates bonds that hold when the lighting is bad, and the angles are unflattering, and life is not cooperating with the aesthetic.

Nature's Way: How the Earth Teaches Love

Have you ever noticed that nature never rushes, yet everything gets done? The trees do not panic about whether spring will come. The rivers do not force their way to the ocean. The flowers do not strain to open; they simply open when the time is right, when the conditions align, when their nature calls them forward.

The seasons do not compete with each other. Winter does not try to be summer. Autumn does not apologize for its falling leaves. Each season fulfills its purpose completely, without trying to be something it is not, without comparing itself to what came before or what will follow.

Even the sun rises slowly. No alarms, no urgency, just divine timing. It does not burst over the horizon in anxious haste. It takes its time, painting the sky in gradual colors, trusting that it will arrive exactly when it is meant to arrive.

Love works the same way. You do not have to force it, manipulating circumstances and people to make it happen. You do not have to chase it, exhausting yourself in pursuit of something that keeps receding. You do not have to dress it up, performing and presenting to deserve it.

You just have to align with it. To become the kind of person who attracts it naturally. To live in such a way that love recognizes you as its home.

Eat like you love your body. Not punishing it with deprivation or drowning it in excess, but nourishing it with intention, honoring it as the home of your soul.

Move like you honor your energy. Not forcing yourself through workouts you hate or sitting in stagnation because movement feels like punishment, but finding ways to inhabit your body fully, to feel alive in your own skin.

Speak like your words plant gardens. Knowing that what you say to yourself and others grows into something. Choose words that cultivate beauty rather than words that spread destruction.

Rest like the world can wait, because your peace cannot. Refusing to sacrifice your well-being on the altar of productivity. Trusting that rest is not laziness but wisdom, not indulgence but necessity.

That is how nature loves us back. When we finally slow down long enough to receive it. When we stop rushing past the beauty, stop forcing the timeline, stop competing with rhythms that were never meant to be hurried.

The Resurrection Within Marriage

I once met a woman who had been married for twenty years. From the outside, her life looked complete. A long marriage. A family built together. A partnership that had weathered decades. But when she spoke, there was a sadness beneath her words that had nothing to do with her husband.

She told me, "I love my husband. That has never been the question. But somewhere between being a wife, a mom, and a business owner, I forgot who I was. I became so defined by my roles that the woman beneath them disappeared. I could not remember what I liked anymore, what I wanted, what made me feel alive outside of serving everyone else."

She did not need to leave her marriage. She did not need a dramatic change of circumstances. She needed to find herself within the life she had built.

She started with something small: walking alone in the park every morning. No headphones filling her ears with other people's voices. No agenda driving her pace. Just her and the sunrise. Just her own thoughts, her own breath, her own company. It felt strange at first, almost uncomfortable, like meeting someone she used to know but had not seen in years.

After a few weeks, something unexpected happened. Her husband asked if he could join her. Not to talk about logistics or problems or the endless details of shared life, but just to walk. Just to be together in a different way than they had been in years.

They started talking. Not about bills or kids or schedules, but about dreams they had forgotten they had. Memories they had not revisited in decades. The people they were before responsibilities piled up and adulthood demanded so much. They were rediscovering each other by first rediscovering themselves.

She said something I will never forget: "I didn't need a new marriage. I needed a new me. And when I found her, everything else started to shift. Not because my husband changed, but because I finally brought my whole self back to our life together."

That is the magic of soulful love. It does not always come from outside. It is not always about finding someone new or changing your circumstances dramatically. Sometimes it is a quiet resurrection of what has been waiting within you all along. Sometimes the revolution is internal. Sometimes coming home to yourself transforms every relationship you are already in.

Spiritual Reflection

True love mirrors the way God loves. Patient, never rushing us toward transformation we are not ready for. Pure, without hidden agendas or manipulative intent. Present, fully here, fully engaged, fully attentive to who we are in this moment.

Divine love does not demand perfection. It invites partnership. It does not require us to be fixed before we are loved but loves us toward our healing. It does not keep score, tallying up our failures to use against us later. It keeps faith, believing in who we are becoming even when we cannot see it ourselves.

"Love is patient, love is kind. It does not envy, it does not boast, it is not proud." (1 Corinthians 13:4)

You were not created to beg for love. You were not designed to earn it through performance or purchase it through sacrifice. You were created to be it. To embody it. To let it flow through you and from you into a world that desperately needs more of it.

And the moment you become soulful in your living, the moment you start treating yourself with the patience and kindness that divine love offers, something shifts. You stop attracting people who feed your insecurities, who keep you small to make themselves feel large, who benefit from your self-doubt. You start attracting those who nourish your peace, who celebrate your growth, who meet your wholeness with their own.

Hard Truths (with a Wink)

He does not need you to fix him, and you do not need him to complete you. Two whole people make better partners than two half people trying to create one whole. Bring your own wholeness.

Pretty will not fix lonely. Alignment will. You can be the most beautiful person in the room and still go home to emptiness. Beauty attracts attention. Alignment attracts connection.

You cannot heal in a relationship that punishes honesty. If telling the truth makes things worse, you are not in a safe space. Healing requires environments where truth is welcomed, not weaponized.

"Being the prize" is not about ego. It is about energy. It is not about thinking you are better than others. It is about knowing your worth and refusing to negotiate it down to make someone comfortable.

Do not look for butterflies. Look for calm. Butterflies live short lives. That flutter in your stomach might be excitement, but it might also be anxiety in disguise. Calm is sustainable. Calm is what lasts.

"If love feels like a competition, you're playing the wrong game."

Journal Prompts

> *What does a "soulful day" look like to me? What elements would be present? What would be absent?*
>
> *How can I make space for love without losing myself? What boundaries would help me stay whole while opening to partnership?*
>
> *What habits, routines, or relationships help me feel grounded and aligned? Which ones deplete me?*
>
> *Where have I been performing rather than being authentic in my approach to love?*

Affirmation

I am rooted, radiant, and real. I give and receive love without performance. I am both soft and strong, and I honor love that feels like peace, not pressure. I attract what I embody. I embody wholeness.

Closing Truth

Soulful love does not make your heart race. It makes it rest. It does not create anxiety masquerading as excitement. It creates calm that feels like coming home.

It is not fireworks. It is a steady flame. Not spectacular displays that burn out quickly, but consistent warmth that sustains through seasons. The kind of fire that keeps you warm rather than burns your house down.

It does not need applause or approval. It does not require an audience to witness it or validation to believe it is real. It just is. Quiet and certain. Present and true.

And when you finally become the kind of woman who lives with intention, laughter, and truth, when you stop performing and start being, when you find your own peace and protect it fiercely—you will not have to search for soulful love.

It will find you. Because you already are. You are the love you have been seeking. You are the peace you have been craving. You are the wholeness you thought someone else would provide.

And from that place of already being, you will attract what matches you. Not what you chase. Not what you perform for. But what recognizes itself in you and moves toward home.

~

Now that we understand what soulful love requires, let us examine what stands in its way: the cultural myths and checklists we must leave behind.

CHAPTER NINE

When the World Forgets What Love Looks Like

"When we stop performing and start healing, the world around us remembers how to love."

Opening Scene

We live in a world obsessed with appearances. Perfect couples smiling from vacation destinations that look like they were designed by an algorithm. Perfect families coordinating outfits for photographs that will be edited, filtered, and posted for strangers to admire. Perfect feeds where everyone's life seems effortless, beautiful, enviable. Scroll through any social platform and you will see a world where everything seems better, brighter, more together than your own.

Everyone is smiling, but nobody is safe. Nobody is showing the argument that happened before the photo was taken. Nobody is revealing the loneliness that exists in the same house as the picture-perfect family. Nobody is talking about the anxiety, the disconnection, the quiet desperation that lives behind the curated image.

We have mistaken performance for purpose, confusing looking good with being good, presenting well with living well. We have mistaken filters for fulfillment, as though the right lighting and the right angle could compensate for emptiness. We have mistaken validation for value, counting likes and comments as though they were currency that could purchase actual worth.

We celebrate curated chaos, calling it "content." We applaud the dramatic reveal, the vulnerable post that is not actually vulnerable but carefully constructed for maximum engagement. We confuse attention with affection, believing that being seen by many is the same as being known by someone. It is not. You can have millions of followers and still feel utterly alone.

And this performance is not limited to social media. It bleeds into every area of our lives. We perform at work, presenting competence when we feel uncertain, projecting confidence when we are drowning. We perform at home, maintaining images of togetherness when relationships are fraying. We perform in friendships, saying "I'm fine" when we are anything but.

We smile through heartbreak because we have been taught that strength means not showing pain. We apologize for being tired, as though needing rest were a character flaw rather than a human necessity. We pretend we are okay so no one asks what is really wrong, because answering that question honestly would require a vulnerability we have learned is dangerous.

But pretending does not heal pain. It hides it. And everything we bury alive will eventually surface, usually through the very people we love the most. The emotions we suppress do not disappear. They find other outlets: passive aggression, physical symptoms, explosive reactions that seem disproportionate to their triggers. Our children absorb what we will not process. Our partners receive the overflow of what we refuse to acknowledge.

The Ripple Effect of Inauthentic Living

When we hide from our truth, our children learn to hide too. They watch us. They absorb our patterns before they have words to describe them. They learn what is acceptable to feel and what must be concealed. They inherit our relationship with honesty, our comfort with vulnerability, our capacity or incapacity for authentic expression. What we model becomes their blueprint.

When we normalize burnout, when we wear exhaustion as a badge of honor and treat rest as weakness, our homes stop feeling like a sanctuary. They become just another place to perform, another stage where we have roles to maintain. The walls that should provide shelter instead witness the same pretense we offer the outside world. Our families do not get our real selves. They get what is left over after we have performed for everyone else.

When we silence our emotions, dismissing our own feelings as inconvenient or inappropriate, we raise generations afraid to speak theirs. Our children learn that some parts of themselves are unacceptable. They learn to fragment, to hide, to present only the portions that will be approved. They inherit our disconnection from ourselves and carry it forward.

Our world is not broken because people stopped loving each other. There is still love. It is everywhere, trying to find expression, trying to connect, trying to heal. Our world is broken because people stopped loving themselves enough to tell the truth. Because authenticity became risky. Because vulnerability was weaponized. Because somewhere along the way, we decided that the appearance of having it together was more important than actually being together, with ourselves and with each other.

Love has become a costume, worn to impress rather than expressed to connect. We put on the outfit of partnership, of family, of friendship, but forget to actually inhabit the relationship. We look like we love without actually loving. We perform intimacy without risking it.

But here is the good news, and it is genuinely good: Healing is contagious too. Just as dysfunction spreads through families and communities, so does wholeness. Just as pretense creates distance, authenticity creates connection. When one person starts to love better, to speak with grace instead of contempt, to pause instead of attack, to listen instead of judge, it changes the emotional temperature of an entire home. One healed person can shift the trajectory of generations.

The Mother Who Stopped Pretending

A woman once told me she used to cry in the shower every morning before waking her kids. She would stand under the hot water, letting her tears mix with the stream, releasing the grief and overwhelm she felt unable to show anywhere else. Then she would step out, wipe her face, apply her makeup like armor, and emerge into her family's day with a smile that suggested everything was fine.

She thought she was protecting them. She thought her pain was hers to carry alone, that burdening her children with her struggles would be unfair, would damage them, would steal their childhood innocence. She believed the best thing she could do was perform stability, even when stability felt impossibly far from her reality.

She did not realize her daughter had noticed. Children see more than we give them credit for. They read the tension in our shoulders. They hear the tears we think we have hidden. They sense the gap between our words and our energy. They know when something is wrong, even when we insist everything is fine.

One day, after an argument about something small that had escalated in the way arguments do when bigger things are brewing underneath, her little girl said something that changed everything. She looked up at her mother with those eyes that see through pretense and said, "Mommy, you don't have to be happy all the time. I love you even when you're sad."

That moment shattered her. Not from shame, though shame tried to enter. From truth. The purest kind of truth that comes from children who have not yet learned to filter reality. Her daughter did not need a perfect mom. She had never asked for one. She needed a present one. A real one. A mother she could actually know, not just a performance she could witness.

So she stopped pretending. Not all at once, not perfectly, but progressively. She cried when she needed to, sometimes in front of her children, naming what she was feeling so they could learn that emotions were information, not emergencies. She apologized when she overreacted, modeling accountability rather than infallibility. She laughed louder, giving herself permission to feel joy as fully as she had hidden pain. She rested more, demonstrating that care for herself was not selfishness but necessity. She prayed deeper, reconnecting with the source of her strength.

And slowly, the home changed. Not because she became flawless. She was still imperfect, still learning, still struggling some days. But because she became real. Because authenticity replaced performance. Because her children finally got to know their actual mother, not the character she had been playing.

Her daughter, watching this transformation, learned something profound: that being human was acceptable. Those feelings could be expressed, and the world would not end. That love did not require pretense. She learned this not from a lecture but from a lived example. She inherited honesty instead of performance.

The True Identity Crisis

What we call a "relationship crisis" is often just a reflection of an identity crisis. The problems that surface between two people frequently have their roots in the problems that exist within each person. We bring our unresolved selves into partnership and wonder why things do not work.

When you do not know who you are, you settle for who others tell you to be. You become whatever seems acceptable, whatever appears lovable, whatever draws approval. You shape-shift to match expectations, losing yourself in the process of trying to be found by someone else. And then you wonder why you feel empty, even in relationships that should fulfill you. How could they fulfill you? They are not connected to the real you. They are connected to a character you created.

When you are disconnected from yourself, you will always feel disconnected in love. The intimacy you crave requires a self to offer. If you do not know that self, if you have lost touch with your own desires and values and truth, you have nothing authentic to bring. You can only offer performance. And performance, no matter how convincing, cannot satisfy the deep human need for genuine connection.

That is why the journey back to self-love is not selfish. It is a social responsibility. It is perhaps the least selfish thing you can do, because a healed you benefits everyone around you.

When you know your worth, you stop creating chaos. You no longer need drama to feel alive, validation to feel valuable, conflict to feel seen. You can exist in peace, which creates peace around you.

When you have compassion for your past, you stop projecting it onto others. You stop seeing threats where there are none, stop punishing present people for past wounds, stop requiring others to carry baggage that is yours to process.

When you take accountability, you stop blaming everyone else for your pain. You own what is yours. You change what you can change. You stop waiting for others to fix what only you can heal.

Healthy individuals create healthy families. They bring their wholeness into their homes, modeling for children what it looks like being at peace with yourself, to process emotions well, to repair after rupture.

Healthy families create healthy communities. They raise children who become adults capable of connection, contribution, and compassion. They send people into the world who know how to love because they were shown how.

Healthy communities build a loving world. One home at a time. One relationship at a time. One person at a time. It all starts with you. Not because you are responsible for fixing everything, but because you are responsible for healing yourself. And that healing ripples outward in ways you may never fully see.

Why Grace Is the New Revolution

Grace is love without judgment. It is the radical acceptance of imperfection, in yourself and in others. It is the ability to say, "I have done better, and I have done worse, and both versions of me are worthy of compassion." It does not excuse harm, but it refuses to define anyone, including yourself, by their worst moments.

In a world that cancels people for past mistakes, that holds grudges as though they were precious possessions, that demands perfection while offering none, grace is revolutionary. It disrupts the cycle of shame and condemnation. It creates space for growth rather than just punishment.

When you start to live with grace toward yourself, everything shifts. You stop shaming yourself for being human. You release the impossible standard of perfection you have been trying to meet. You acknowledge your flaws without being destroyed by them. You learn from your failures without being defined by them.

You forgive faster. Not because forgiveness is always deserved, but because holding resentment costs you more than releasing it. You understand that forgiveness is not about the other person. It is about freeing yourself from the prison of bitterness.

You listen deeper. Grace creates curiosity instead of condemnation. When someone behaves in ways you do not understand, instead of immediately judging, you wonder what might be happening beneath the surface. You remember that everyone is carrying something.

You lead with empathy, not ego. Your need to be right becomes less important than your desire to understand. Your need to win arguments fades in the face of your need to preserve connection. You care more about people than positions.

And that is how real transformation begins. Not through rules that constrain from the outside in. Not through roles that define you by function rather than identity. But through relationships healed from the inside out. Through the radical practice of grace that changes how you see yourself and therefore how you see everyone else.

Fifteen Years of Grace

I once met a couple who had been married for fifteen years. When I say "survived," I mean it literally. They had been through things that end most marriages. Betrayal that shattered trust. Grief that left them hollowed out. Financial struggle that added stress to an already strained relationship. And the silent seasons, perhaps the hardest of all, when love felt more like duty than desire, when they stayed because they had committed to stay, not because staying felt good.

When I asked what kept them together through all of it, expecting perhaps a romantic answer about undying passion, the wife said something simpler and more profound: "Grace. Not feelings. Grace."

She smiled, that knowing smile of someone who has earned wisdom through pain, and added, "We stopped trying to win arguments. We started trying to understand each other. Once we did that, everything changed."

Their secret was not perfection. It was honesty. They had learned that pretending was more dangerous than truth, that sweeping things under rugs only created bumpy floors, that the pain of honest conversation was less than the pain of accumulated resentment.

They did not post couple selfies every week. They were not performing their relationship for an audience. They were too busy building a friendship, the kind of friendship that could hold the weight of hard days, that could survive disappointment, that could forgive and repair and keep choosing each other.

And that is the truth most people miss: The loudest love stories online are often the quietest behind closed doors. The couples posting most frequently are sometimes the ones struggling most privately. The image rarely matches reality.

And the quietest love stories are usually the most rooted in truth. The ones you never hear about because they do not need an audience. The ones built on daily choices rather than dramatic gestures. The ones sustained by grace rather than feelings, by commitment rather than convenience.

Breaking the Cycle of Drama and Trauma

Every family has a pattern. Some patterns are obvious, loud, impossible to ignore. The yelling that echoes through generations. The addiction that passes from parent to child. The violence that repeats because no one taught anything different. Some patterns are quieter, more subtle, but no less powerful. The emotional unavailability. The perfectionism. The silent treatment. The conflict avoidance that leaves everything unresolved. The sweeping of things under rugs that creates homes full of invisible debris.

Some families throw rugs across rooms. Others sweep everything beneath them. Neither approach heals. Both pass pain forward.

But someone has to stop it. Someone has to look at the pattern, recognize it for what it is, and say, "This ends with me." Not because they are better than those who came before. Those who came before were doing their best with what they had, passing on what they received, surviving the only way they knew how. But because someone has to be the one who learns a different way. Someone has to break the chain.

When you choose healing over habit, you disrupt generations of dysfunction. You take what was automatic and make it conscious. You examine what was inherited and decide what to keep and what to release.

When you choose forgiveness over resentment, you free yourself and everyone connected to you. The bitterness you refuse to carry cannot be passed to your children. The grudge you release cannot poison your relationships.

When you choose reflection over reaction, you create space between stimulus and response. You stop the automatic patterns that would otherwise perpetuate. You respond from intention rather than inheritance.

You are rewriting your family's emotional DNA. You are changing what gets passed forward. You are giving your children, your friends, even your coworkers permission to breathe differently. To feel differently. To respond differently. They see you breaking the pattern, and they learn that patterns can be broken.

The New Definition of Legacy

Legacy is not what you leave in your bank account. It is not the assets you accumulate, the properties you acquire, the inheritance you pass down. Those things may matter, but they are not legacy. Not really. Not in the way that shapes generations.

Legacy is what you leave in people's hearts. It is the imprint you make on souls. It is the way you change people simply by being yourself, by loving them, by showing up in their lives with presence and truth.

Legacy is how your children remember your tone of voice. Not the words you said, which they may forget, but the way those words felt. Were you harsh or gentle? Impatient or understanding? Did your voice feel like criticism or like home?

Legacy is how your partner recalls your patience. The moments when you could have reacted but chose to pause. The times when you were frustrated but chose kindness anyway. The way you made them feel valued even on difficult days.

Legacy is the way your presence makes people feel. Safe, seen, and understood. Or anxious, invisible, and alone. People may not remember what you said or did, but they will remember how you made them feel. That feeling is your legacy.

When you love yourself better, you raise the standard of love everywhere you go. You create homes that feel like healing, where people can come as they are and be received with grace. You create workplaces that feel like teamwork, where people collaborate rather than compete, where humanity is honored alongside productivity. You create friendships that feel like sanctuary, where truth can be spoken and hearts can rest.

That is not just personal growth. That is social transformation. One person healing, then creating environments where others can heal. One person choosing differently, then inspiring others to examine their own choices. The ripple expands from your healing outward, touching lives you may never know you reached.

Spiritual Reflection

Even Jesus did not perform His worth. He embodied it. He did not try to convince people of His value through spectacle or debate. He simply was who He was, and that presence spoke for itself.

He did not chase applause. The crowds came and went. Sometimes they worshipped Him; sometimes they wanted to kill Him. His sense of identity did not fluctuate with their approval. He served with authenticity regardless of how it was received.

He did not force people to believe. He invited them to experience love through truth. He offered Himself and allowed people the freedom to respond. There was no manipulation, no coercion, no performance designed to create a specific outcome. Just truth, offered freely.

"Let all that you do be done in love." (1 Corinthians 16:14)

When we live from love, not from performance or pride, we mirror heaven on Earth. We become expressions of divine love in human form. We demonstrate what is possible when a person stops striving for approval and starts living from identity.

Hard Truths (with Humor and Humanity)

Pretending is expensive. It costs you peace. Every performance requires energy that could have gone toward something real. Every mask requires maintenance. The bill always comes due.

You cannot post your way into purpose. No amount of perfectly curated content creates meaning. No number of likes fills the void of unlived life. Put down the phone and pick up your actual existence.

Drama might get you attention, but peace will keep you whole. The chaos that makes for interesting stories makes for exhausting lives. Choose boring if boring means stable. Choose quiet if quiet means sane.

Love is not loud. Insecurity is. The people yelling about how much they love often love the least. Real love does not need to announce itself. It simply shows up, consistently, without fanfare.

You cannot build healthy children in homes that reward silence and punish emotion. They will learn what you model. If you teach them that feelings are dangerous, they will grow up disconnected from themselves. Give them permission to feel by feeling yourself.

"When you love yourself, you stop teaching others how to live in dysfunction."

Journal Prompts

What does authenticity look like in my daily life, not my online life? Where is the gap between what I present and what I experience?

What habits, people, or performances drain my peace the most? What would it cost to release them?

What emotional inheritance do I want my children or community to receive from me? What am I currently passing on?

Where am I performing instead of being present? What would change if I stopped?

Affirmation

I no longer perform for love. I lead with grace, truth, and compassion. I am rewriting the story, one honest act, one healed moment, one loving word at a time. My authenticity gives others permission to be real.

Closing Truth

When we heal, the world heals a little too. Not dramatically, not all at once, but incrementally. One person at a time. One relationship at a time. One home at a time. Your healing is not just about you. It is about everyone your life touches.

When we choose peace, our children breathe easier. They absorb the calm we cultivate. They learn that life does not have to be constant chaos. They inherit our wholeness instead of our wounds.

When we tell the truth, others find the courage to stop pretending. They see us being real and realize it is possible. They see us surviving authenticity and begin to believe they might survive it too. Our honesty gives them permission.

You are not just breaking patterns. You are building a new world. One rooted in authenticity rather than performance. In empathy rather than judgment. In grace rather than condemnation.

And maybe that is what love has been trying to teach us all along. That it was never about finding the perfect person or creating the perfect image. It was about becoming real. About telling the truth. About healing ourselves so we could stop hurting others.

When we love ourselves better, we give the whole world permission to do the same. One healed heart at a time. One honest conversation at a time. One moment of grace at a time. The revolution starts within. And it spreads from there.

~

Now that we understand the world we are healing, let us explore what we are building: partnership that moves us from survival to soulmate.

CHAPTER TEN

From Survival to Soulmate

"You don't find your soulmate. You become your own first, and then love recognizes you."

Opening Scene

No one ever taught us that love would require this much self-awareness. The fairy tales never mentioned the inner work. The romantic comedies skipped the therapy scenes. The love songs did not include verses about attachment styles and trigger management and the slow, unglamorous work of becoming someone capable of healthy partnership.

We were told to find "the one." As if there were a single person somewhere on this planet destined for us, and our job was simply to locate them. As if love were a treasure hunt rather than a construction project. As if the finding were the hard part, and everything after would be effortless.

No one told us how to become “the one”. No one explained that the quality of love we could receive was directly connected to the quality of love we had cultivated within ourselves. No one mentioned that we might need to heal, to grow, to transform before we would be ready to recognize the love that was looking for us.

But what if soulmates are not people we meet by fate, crossed paths written in stars before we were born? What if they are mirrors that reveal our faith? Reflections of the work we have done, the healing we have embraced, the wholeness we have cultivated?

What if every connection, every heartbreak, every misunderstanding, every relationship that did not work out, was life's way of asking a simple question: "Will you choose love again, starting with you?" Will you keep opening? Will you keep growing? Will you keep becoming the person who can receive what you are asking for?

Because here is the truth that no one advertises: No one can perfect self-love. There is no graduation ceremony. No moment when you arrive and the work is complete. It is not a finish line to cross but a lifelong relationship to tend. A relationship with yourself, with your Creator, and with everyone who crosses your path.

The Illusion of "Healed People Only"

We have created a strange standard in the modern love world. A prerequisite that sounds wise but is actually impossible. "Do not date unless you are healed." "You have to love yourself completely before anyone else can love you." "Get your house in order before you invite anyone in."

But if that were literally true, if complete healing were required before partnership could begin, we would all be single until the second coming. Because healing is not a destination. It is a direction. We are all works in progress, all somewhere on the journey, all carrying wounds that surface at unexpected moments.

Healing is not a prerequisite for love. It is a process within it. The relationship itself becomes a container for growth, a context where healing continues. Love has a way of revealing what still needs attention, of surfacing what we thought we had resolved, of inviting us into deeper layers of our own becoming.

The goal is not to find someone flawless. That person does not exist. The goal is to find someone faithful enough to grow beside you. Someone committed to their own healing while supporting yours. Someone who can hold space for your imperfection while working on their own.

Some days you will be the teacher, the one with wisdom to offer, the one whose clarity illuminates confusion. Other days you will be the student, humbled by your own blind spots, grateful for a partner who can see what you cannot.

Some days your partner's strength will carry you. They will be the steady one while you fall apart, the anchor while you are tossed by storms. Other days, your peace will anchor them. They will need your stability while they navigate their own chaos.

That is partnership. Not perfection. Two imperfect people committed to the same direction. Two healing people choosing to heal together. Two growing people who believe the other is worth growing for.

When Love Became a Mirror

I once had a relationship that was nothing like the chaos I had known before. For years, my romantic history had been marked by intensity that I mistook for passion, by drama that I confused with depth, by the kind of love that left me exhausted and empty and wondering if I was fundamentally unlovable.

This was different. There was safety in it. The kind of safety that allowed me to exhale, to stop performing, to show up without the armor I had learned to wear. There was care, genuine care that showed up in actions, not just words. And there was honesty, sometimes too honest, the kind of transparency that left nowhere to hide.

But even in that safety, fear showed up. Not fear of them, because they had given me no reason to fear. Fear of myself. Fear of losing myself again, of disappearing into another person the way I had before, of abandoning my own center to merge with someone else. And I could see the same fear in their eyes, the same hesitation, the same protective caution born of past wounds.

We realized we were being tested. Not by each other. Neither of us was creating obstacles or playing games. We were being tested by our own growth. By the healing we had done and the healing that remained. By the question of whether we could apply what we had learned.

Could we love without disappearing? Could we be intimate without abandoning ourselves? Could we be vulnerable without losing our footing? Could we stay rooted in who we were while opening to someone else?

That relationship did not end because it was bad. There was nothing wrong with it. It evolved because it revealed who we were becoming. It showed us parts of ourselves we had not fully seen before. It accomplished what it was meant to accomplish, and then it completed.

It taught me something I had never understood: Love is not supposed to complete you. That is too much pressure to place on another person. Love is supposed to meet you. To find you where you already are, already whole, already becoming. It adds to your life; it does not become your life.

Love as a Mirror, Not a Medicine

Romantic love is often where our deepest wounds show up. This is not a flaw in the design. It is a feature. Because romantic love is where we are most vulnerable, most exposed, most unable to maintain the defenses we carry everywhere else. And vulnerability, as uncomfortable as it can be, is also where we are most free. Free to be seen. Free to be known. Free to discover what we have been hiding even from ourselves.

The people we attract are rarely random. They are living lessons walking into our lives at precisely the moment we need what they have to teach. They reflect our confidence back to us, showing us where we stand strong. They reflect our fears, surfacing anxieties we thought we had conquered. They reflect our healing, demonstrating how far we have come. And they reflect our hidden pain, revealing wounds we did not know were still bleeding.

When you meet someone kind who still triggers your insecurities, that is not sabotage. That is not evidence that something is wrong with the relationship or with you. That is your heart saying, "Here is another layer to love. Here is more healing available. Here is deeper work that only intimacy could have revealed."

Love does not expose us to shame. It is not meant to make us feel worse about ourselves, to remind us of our inadequacy, to punish us for not being further along. Love exposes us to truth. And that truth, however uncomfortable it may be to face, is what sets us free. We cannot heal what we cannot see. Love helps us see.

For the Women: Release the War, Return to Wonder

Many women today carry quiet fatigue. Not just from relationships, though relationships have certainly contributed. But from the constant performance of strength. From the pressure to be everything, to handle everything, to need nothing and no one. From surviving heartbreak with hustle, as though productivity could compensate for pain. From responding to rejection with fierce independence, as though needing connection were weakness. From meeting disappointment with detachment, as though numbness were the same as healing.

We have learned to armor ourselves so effectively that sometimes we forget we are wearing armor. We have become so skilled at being strong that we have lost touch with what it feels like to be soft. We have protected ourselves so thoroughly that we have also imprisoned ourselves, safe from harm but also unable to receive tenderness.

But true power is not in becoming harder. It is not in building higher walls, thicker armor, more impenetrable defenses. True power is in becoming whole. In integrating all parts of yourself, the strong and the soft, the capable and the vulnerable, the independent and the longing for connection.

Loving yourself does not mean swearing off love. It does not mean giving up on partnership or deciding that you are better off alone. And it certainly does not mean distrusting all men, painting half the population with the brush of your worst experiences.

Loving yourself means letting love find you without requiring it to fix you. Coming to partnership already whole, already valuable, already enough. Not looking for someone to complete you but for someone to complement you. Not seeking rescue but seeking companionship.

You can be both soft and smart. These are not contradictions. You can feel deeply and think clearly. You can be tender and strategic. You can let your guard down without losing your discernment.

You can have standards without walls. Knowing what you want and require is not the same as being closed off. You can be selective without being defended. You can protect yourself without isolating yourself.

You can lead without losing your femininity. Leadership and femininity are not opposites. You can be powerful and graceful. You can make decisions and remain soft. You can take charge and still receive.

And yes, you can let a good man love you without thinking you have lost your edge. Receiving love is not weakness. Being cared for is not regression. Allowing someone to contribute to your life is not dependency. It is the natural flow of a healthy partnership.

For the Men: You Are Needed, Too

Men are not the enemy. They are not the villains of every love story gone wrong. They are not a monolith to be blamed for collective sins. They are individuals, as varied and complex as women, carrying their own wounds, fighting their own battles, longing for their own healing. They are the other half of the lesson, essential partners in the dance of love that requires two.

A healed man is not a myth. He is not a unicorn that exists only in imagination. He exists in the real world, walking among us, working on himself, growing into who he was meant to be. He exists not because he is perfect, not because he has eliminated all his flaws, but because he is aware. Aware of his patterns. Aware of his wounds. Aware of the impact he has on others. And committed to growth.

The healed man is learning how to feel without shame. He is unlearning the messages that told him emotions were weakness, that vulnerability was danger, that real men do not cry. He is discovering that his feelings are information, not enemies. That accessing his emotional world makes him more capable, not less.

He is learning to protect without pride. To use his strength in service of those he loves rather than in service of his ego. To be strong without being dominating. To provide safety without requiring submission.

He is learning to provide without control. To contribute without keeping score. To give without expecting a return on investment. To support without strings attached.

He wants peace, not performance. He is tired of relationships that feel like battlegrounds, tired of proving himself, tired of the games that pass for connection. He wants a home where he can rest, where his presence is valued, where he does not have to fight to be seen.

He wants respect, not worship. He does not need to be placed on a pedestal or treated as superior. He needs to be honored for who he is, to feel that his contributions matter, to know that his presence makes a difference.

He wants softness, not submission. He does not need a woman who abandons herself to please him.

He needs a partner who brings her own fullness, her own opinions, her own desires. He wants her surrender to be a choice made from safety, not a requirement enforced by fear.

Men also feel unseen. They just hide it differently. Behind silence that gets read as coldness. Behind sarcasm that masks pain. Behind busyness that creates distance. They struggle too, with identity in a world that sends conflicting messages about what masculinity means. With purpose in an economy that often values them only for production. With wanting to lead in a culture that sometimes calls healthy leadership dominance, and wanting to love in a culture that sometimes calls emotional availability weakness.

But when a man feels trusted, truly trusted, believed in, relied upon, something in him softens. He becomes tender in ways he could not be while defending himself. He opens in ways he could not while proving himself.

When he feels respected, honored for who he is and what he brings, he becomes receptive. He can hear feedback without defensiveness. He can receive direction without feeling controlled.

And when he feels emotionally safe, when he knows he can be vulnerable without it being weaponized, when he knows his struggles will be met with compassion rather than contempt, he becomes unstoppable. Not in an aggressive way, but in a generative way. He pours himself into building, creating, providing, loving.

Because love heals him, too. Not just her. Not just the women who have been wounded by love gone wrong. Him, too. The man who has been hardened by rejection. The man who has been criticized into silence. The man who has been treated as a utility rather than a human. Love heals him when it finally arrives in a form he can trust.

The Dance of Dual Healing

A soulmate connection is not two people who never argue. That is not intimacy; that is avoidance. It is two people who know how to argue. Who can engage in conflict without destroying each other. Who fight with grace, managing their own reactivity, staying present even when emotions run high. Who apologize without ego, releasing the need to be right in favor of the need to be connected.

They see the wound beneath the reaction. When their partner says something hurtful, they look beyond the words to the pain that prompted them. They ask not "How could you say that?" but "What are you feeling that made those words come out?" They recognize that attack often comes from fear, that criticism often comes from hurt, that withdrawal often comes from overwhelm.

In conscious love, you stop asking "Who is right?" That question is a dead end. Someone wins, someone loses, and the relationship suffers regardless of the verdict. Instead, you ask "What are we both trying to protect?" What need is driving my position? What fear is fueling yours? When you understand the underlying needs, solutions become possible that satisfy both.

Every argument becomes a conversation. Not a battle to be won but an exploration to be navigated together. Every silence becomes an invitation. Not a punishment or a wall but an opportunity to create space and return with more clarity. Every trigger becomes a teacher. Not evidence that you chose wrong but information about what still needs healing.

That is not a weakness. That is wisdom. The wisdom to know that connection matters more than winning. That understanding matters more than agreement. That two people who can navigate conflict well will go further than two people who never conflict at all.

Words That Build Bridges: Communication Scripts

Learning to communicate needs and boundaries is not just about knowing what you want. It is about knowing how to express it in ways that invite connection rather than create walls. Here are some scripts that can help you navigate difficult conversations:

When you need to set a boundary:

Instead of: "You always..." or "You never..." (which triggers defensiveness)

Try: "I've noticed that when [specific behavior] happens, I feel [emotion]. What I need is [clear request]. Can we talk about how to make that work for both of us?"

When you are feeling triggered:

Instead of: Reacting immediately or shutting down

Try: "I'm having a strong reaction right now, and I want to respond thoughtfully rather than reactively. Can I have a few minutes to process, and then let's talk about this?"

When you need to express a need:

Instead of: Hoping they will figure it out or hinting

Try: "Something that would really help me feel loved and connected is [specific action]. Would you be open to that?"

When you need to address a pattern:

Instead of: "This keeps happening and I'm fed up"

Try: "I've noticed a pattern that's affecting me. Can we find time to talk about it together? I want to understand your perspective too."

When you need to repair after conflict:

Instead of: Pretending it did not happen or waiting for them to apologize first

Try: "I want to come back to what happened earlier. I value our relationship too much to let that sit between us. Can we talk about how we both felt and what we each need going forward?"

The key is speaking from your own experience ("I feel," "I need") rather than making accusations about their character ("You are," "You always"). This creates space for them to hear you without needing to defend themselves.

The Man Who Finally Felt Seen

A man once told me, "I didn't know how much I needed emotional safety until I finally had it." He had spent his entire adult life believing that strength meant stoicism, that being a good partner meant fixing problems, that his value was in his solutions, not his presence.

He said he used to shut down every time his partner cried. Not because he did not care. He cared deeply, which was precisely the problem. Her tears made him feel powerless. He could not fix tears. He could not solve sadness. And if he could not fix it, he did not know what to do. So he froze. He withdrew. He went silent when she most needed him to be present.

Then one day, she said something that changed everything. She looked at him through her tears and said simply, "You don't have to fix me. Just stay."

He did. He stayed. He did not offer solutions. He did not try to cheer her up or change the subject or make the discomfort go away. He just sat with her, present in her pain, offering nothing but his presence.

And something shifted in him. A tightness he had carried for years began to release. A pressure he had not even known he was under started to lift.

He told me later, "For the first time, I realized that being her peace didn't mean solving her pain. It meant standing beside it. It meant not running from it. It meant trusting that my presence was enough, even when I had no answers."

That is the kind of love that changes the world. Not grand gestures that look impressive but leave people feeling unseen. Grounded presence. The willingness to stay when staying is uncomfortable. The choice to be present without needing to perform. The understanding that sometimes the greatest gift we can give is simply to remain.

Soulmates Are Not Fantasy: They Are Frequency

You cannot call in love from fear. You cannot attract partnership while radiating desperation. You cannot draw someone healthy toward you while broadcasting the frequency of your wounds. You attract what your heart is ready to host. What your spirit is prepared to receive. What your life has made space for.

Soulmates do not appear because you have finally figured it all out. They do not arrive as a reward for completing your healing or as a prize for becoming perfect. They appear because you are finally authentic enough to meet someone else who is. Because you have stopped performing and started being. Because your realness can recognize their realness.

It is not fireworks. That is the hardest part for some people to accept. After years of confusing intensity with depth, the real thing can feel anticlimactic at first. It is not the stomach-dropping rush of uncertainty. It is recognition. A quiet knowing. A sense of familiarity that has nothing to do with having met before.

Not "I've been waiting for you," as though you were incomplete until they arrived. But "I remember you," as though some part of your soul recognized some part of theirs. As though you had been walking toward each other all along, and this meeting was inevitable once you both became who you were meant to be.

That is what alignment feels like. Peace, not panic. Recognition, not obsession. Home, not conquest.

Spiritual Reflection

God does not send perfect partners. That would be too easy, and it would not serve our growth. He sends purpose partners. People who stretch you beyond your comfort zone. People who soften your hard edges. People who sanctify the parts of you that still need light, that still need attention, that still need love.

"As iron sharpens iron, so one person sharpens another." (Proverbs 27:17)

The sharpening is not always comfortable. Iron against iron creates friction, heat, sparks. But it also creates a finer edge. A more useful tool. A more refined instrument. The right partner will sharpen you, and that sharpening will sometimes be uncomfortable. But it will also make you better. More fully yourself. More capable of the life you were meant to live.

When you stop trying to find the "perfect match" and start becoming one, everything shifts. You stop looking for someone without flaws and start looking for someone whose flaws you can work with. You stop seeking perfection and start seeking growth.

And love no longer feels like a test you might fail. It becomes a ministry. A service you offer. A gift you give. A calling you fulfill. Not performance for approval, but presence for purpose.

Hard Truths (Softly Spoken)

Healing does not make you ready for love. It makes you responsible for it. You will still have triggers.

You will still have wounds. But you will know how to manage them. You will take ownership of your reactions. You will do the work instead of expecting your partner to do it for you.

Attraction gets your attention. Alignment keeps your peace. The person who makes your heart race is not necessarily the person who can make your heart rest. Choose rest over race.

Every relationship is either a classroom or a celebration, sometimes both on the same day. Some relationships exist primarily to teach you something you need to learn. Others exist to celebrate what you have become. Most do some of each.

If love keeps revealing the same wounds, it is not punishment. It is an invitation. The same wound surfacing again and again is not evidence that you are failing. It is evidence that there is more healing available. Deeper layers. Subtler patterns. The wound keeps appearing because you are finally ready to heal it fully.

"The goal isn't to find someone who completes you. It's to remember you were already whole when you met."

JOURNAL PROMPTS

What do my closest relationships reveal about how I love myself? What patterns do I see?

When I feel triggered in a relationship, what might that moment be trying to teach me? What wound is being surfaced?

How can I bring more understanding and less judgment to both women and men in my life?

What communication pattern do I most need to work on? Which script from this chapter could help?

Affirmation

I am in divine partnership with myself, with others, and with truth. Every person I meet is either teaching me love or reflecting it back. I do not chase connections. I cultivate it. I am already whole, and I welcome a partnership that celebrates that wholeness.

Closing Truth

We all want a love that feels like home. A place where we can rest. A presence where we can breathe. A connection where we can finally stop performing and simply be.

But that home is built from the inside out. It is not something we find ready-made, waiting for us to move in. It is something we construct, brick by brick, choice by choice, day by day.

Every healed boundary adds a brick. Every soft apology that prioritizes connection over ego adds another. Every honest word, spoken with courage and received with grace, adds one more. The home is built through the daily, humble practice of learning how to love.

And when two people bring their authentic selves to the same table, not perfect but present, not complete but committed, they build something even heaven smiles at. Something that glorifies the love that made them both. Something that becomes a sanctuary for everyone who enters it.

Because soulmate love is not found in fairy tales. It is not written in stars that predetermine destiny. It is found in the daily, humble practice of learning, forgiving, growing, and choosing again. It is built by two people who refuse to give up on themselves or each other.

And sometimes, the greatest soulmate you will ever meet is the version of you who finally stopped surviving and started becoming. The one who stopped waiting to be saved and started saving herself. The one who stopped searching for home and realized she had been carrying it within her all along.

She is your first soulmate. Love her well. And watch how the world responds.

~

Now that we understand what soulmate love requires, let us explore the legacy we leave: the lasting impact of loving well.

CHAPTER ELEVEN

Love Is the Oxygen: A Return to the Heart

"You cannot pour from an empty soul. You cannot heal the world while running on fumes. Put on your love first, then help others breathe again."

The Airplane Rule for the Soul

They tell you on every flight, in that safety demonstration that most people ignore while scrolling through their phones: in the event of an emergency, put your oxygen mask on first before helping others.

It sounds selfish the first time you hear it. Your instinct rebels. What kind of person secures their own mask while a child beside them struggles? What kind of mother, what kind of partner, what kind of decent human being tends to themselves while someone they love cannot breathe?

Until you understand the logic. Until you realize that you cannot help anyone if you have lost consciousness. That your unconscious body becomes a burden rather than a help. That in trying to be selfless, you have made yourself useless.

It is not selfishness. It is survival. And beyond survival, it is service. You put your mask on first so you can actually show up for the people who need you. So you can be present rather than passed out. So your help is help and not just intention.

The same rule applies to love. The same logic holds. The same wisdom is needed.

You cannot love your children well if you are constantly running on guilt. If every parenting decision comes from obligation rather than overflow, from depletion rather than abundance, your children feel it. They do not receive love; they receive transactions. They learn that love means losing yourself, and that is not the lesson you want to teach.

You cannot love your partner deeply if you are gasping for emotional air. If every interaction is strained by exhaustion, if every conversation happens on your last nerve, if you have nothing left to give because you have given everything to everyone else, your partnership suffers. Your partner does not get your best. They get your remnants.

You cannot pour into your purpose when your own well is bone dry. The vision that once excited you becomes a burden. The calling that once inspired you becomes a chore. You go through the motions because you committed to them, but the life has drained out of the living.

Love is not self-sacrifice. That is what we were taught, but it was a distortion. Love is self-sustenance. It starts with a full cup, an oxygenated soul, a heart that has received before it tries to give. You first. Then the world. Not because you matter more, but because you matter enough to matter to others.

The Forgotten Language of Love

Love used to be an action. A verb that required movement. Something you did, not just something you felt or said. It showed up in sacrifices that cost something. In presence that required time. In attention that was not divided between the person in front of you and the device in your pocket.

Now it is often a hashtag. A lifestyle brand. A soundbite designed for maximum engagement with minimum requirement. We have reduced love to content, packaged it for consumption, optimized it for algorithms. We speak the word constantly while practicing it rarely.

We say "love" in captions but carry judgment in our tone. The same fingers that type words of affirmation scroll past people in need. The same voice that posts about compassion speaks harshly to the server who got the order wrong. The gap between our public proclamations and our private practices has become a canyon.

We talk about "community" but gossip about our neighbors. We use the language of togetherness while tearing others down in group chats. We celebrate connection in theory while practicing isolation in reality.

We preach "peace" but practice burnout. We post quotes about rest while glorifying exhaustion. We talk about boundaries while ignoring our own. We have become fluent in the vocabulary of wellness while living in a constant state of depletion.

The world does not need more words about love. It has plenty of words. What it needs are living examples. People who walk with kindness when no one is watching. People who speak with patience when it would be easier to snap. People who remember that dignity is a birthright, not a luxury reserved for those who have earned it or who look like us or who agree with us.

Let us make love with truth trendy again. Let us bring back the practice of love that requires something of us. Let us close the gap between what we say and what we do, between what we post and how we live.

The Woman Who Found Her Heart Again

A woman once told me she had spent years chasing love, success, and validation. Running from one accomplishment to the next, one relationship to the next, one achievement to the next. Always reaching. Always striving. Always arriving at destinations that turned out to be just more starting points.

Somewhere in between the chase and the capture, she lost her laughter. Not all at once. Gradually. The way you do not notice weight gain until your clothes no longer fit. One day she realized she could not remember the last time she had laughed until her stomach hurt. Could not recall the last time joy had surprised her.

One afternoon, she was sitting at a café doing what she always did: answering emails, planning the next thing, using every spare moment for productivity. But something made her look up from her phone. Two elderly women at a nearby table were sharing coffee and jokes, their conversation punctuated by laughter that drew the attention of other patrons.

Their eyes were wrinkled. Not from worry, though surely, they had worried. Not from stress, though surely, they had known stress. From joy. From decades of smiling. From a lifetime of finding things funny, of not taking everything so seriously, of letting laughter be a regular visitor rather than a rare guest.

Something in her heart whispered, "That's it."

Not the fame she had chased. Not the followers she had accumulated. Not the fancy life she had constructed, impressive to look at from the outside, exhausting to maintain from within. Just that simple, sacred ability to feel alive in ordinary moments. To find joy in coffee with a friend. To laugh until your eyes crinkle. To be present in the unremarkable Tuesday that would never make a highlight reel but was, in fact, your actual life.

So she began again. Not from scratch, because nothing is ever truly from scratch. But from intention. From a decision to live differently.

She took long walks without earbuds, without podcasts optimizing her time, just her and her thoughts and the world around her. She ate slower, actually tasting her food instead of treating meals as fuel for the next task. She forgave faster, releasing grievances that had been costing her more than they were costing the people she held them against.

She stopped curating her life for external consumption and started living it for internal nourishment. She discovered that an undocumented moment could still be meaningful. That joy did not require an audience. That the best parts of life often happened when the camera was put away.

That is what love looks like when it comes home. Peaceful. Grounded. Real. Not the dramatic, cinematic version that makes for good content. The quiet version that makes for a good life.

A Love That Looks Like Humanity

When you love yourself deeply, something counterintuitive happens. Your heart gets bigger, not smaller. Self-love does not make you more self-absorbed. It makes you more capable of seeing others. Because you are no longer operating from a deficit, from the desperate need to get something, you can finally give something freely.

You stop seeing people as threats or categories. Not competitors for limited resources of love or validation. Not labels to be sorted and evaluated. You start seeing stories. Histories. Struggles. Hopes. You start seeing humans where before you saw stereotypes.

Different cultures become colors, not conflicts. The variety of human expression becomes beautiful rather than threatening. The way others live, worship, celebrate, and grieve becomes fascinating rather than suspicious. You can appreciate the difference without feeling diminished by it.

Different religions become languages, not walls. Different ways of reaching for the divine, of making meaning, of seeking transcendence. Not evidence of who is right and who is wrong, but evidence of humanity's universal longing for something greater than itself.

Different races become reflections of God's creativity, not competition for worth. The vast spectrum of human appearance becomes testimony to divine imagination, not a hierarchy to be defended or resented. Everyone is made in the same image, expressed through infinite variety.

Love becomes less about who is "right" and more about who is willing to see and honor another person's truth. Less about winning arguments and more about building bridges. Less about being correct and more about being kind.

Because everyone you meet is fighting a silent battle. Everyone. The person who cut you off in traffic. The colleague who seems cold. The family member who frustrates you. The stranger who does not smile back. They are all carrying something. They are all struggling with something. They are all hurting in ways that are not visible.

And sometimes the most spiritual thing you can do, more spiritual than any ritual or practice or proclamation, is simply choose kindness. Again and again. In moments when it is easy and moments when it is hard. Toward people who deserve it and people who may not. Kindness as a discipline. Kindness as a spiritual practice. Kindness as love in action.

What It Means to Be Love in a World That Forgets Itself

Being love does not mean being perfect. It does not require flawlessness or sainthood or the elimination of all your rough edges. It means being present. Showing up. Offering your attention, your care, your humanity, even when you are still a work in progress.

It is holding the door for someone having a bad day. A small act that costs you nothing but might remind them that kindness exists. That they are seen. That the world is not as cold as it sometimes seems.

It is smiling at the cashier who has been ignored all morning. Who has rung up transaction after transaction without anyone making eye contact. Who has become invisible in their own workspace. Your smile might be the first genuine human connection they have had in hours.

It is saying "thank you" and meaning it. Not the automatic response that requires no thought, but the genuine acknowledgment of what someone has done for you. The pause to actually appreciate rather than just move on to the next thing.

It is calling your parents, not just texting them. Using your voice. Making the effort that a text does not require. Giving them the sound of you, not just the words.

It is forgiving your own reflection before posting your highlight reel. Accepting the face that looks back at you, unfiltered and unedited, before you show the world the curated version. Loving the real before you present the polished.

When we return to love, when we practice it rather than just preach it, the world softens. Our corner of it, at least. The spaces we inhabit. The people we touch. We stop judging so quickly, releasing the constant evaluation that keeps us separate. We start listening with our hearts, not just our ears, hearing what people mean, not just what they say.

We stop taking everything personally, recognizing that most of what people do has nothing to do with us. We start taking responsibility for the energy we bring, acknowledging that we contribute to the atmosphere of every room we enter.

Love is not complicated. We just got too distracted to notice it. Too busy to practice it. Too defended to receive it. The love that can change the world is not the dramatic, heroic kind. It is the daily, ordinary kind. The kind that shows up in small moments. The kind that anyone can offer. The kind that starts with being present.

The Man Who Learned to Love Beyond Romance

There was once a man who admitted that he used to only express love through grand gestures. Flowers on anniversaries. Expensive dinners for special occasions. Gifts that announced his affection through price tags. He thought that was what love looked like. That was what the movies showed. That was what impressed people.

But then life humbled him. Not through one dramatic event, but through an accumulation of losses. Grief that hollowed him out. Financial struggle that stripped away the resources for grand gestures. The slow erosion of everything he had used to prove his love.

And in that humbling, he learned something he could not have learned any other way: love was not something you bought. It was something you became. It was not measured in dollars or demonstrated through purchases. It was expressed through presence, through words, through showing up.

He began volunteering at a shelter. Not for recognition, not for tax deductions, but because he finally understood that his love was meant to extend beyond his immediate circle. That he had something to offer beyond his earning capacity.

He checked on old friends. Reached out to people he had not contacted in years. Not because he needed anything from them, but because connection itself was the point. Because relationships required tending, and he had let too many wither from neglect.

He learned to say "I'm proud of you" to his son. Words he had never heard from his own father. Words that felt awkward in his mouth at first, unfamiliar terrain, but that his son received like water in a desert.

He learned to say "I need you" to his wife. The hardest words for a man taught that needing was weakness. But when he finally said them, when he finally admitted that she was essential to his life, not just pleasant but necessary, something opened between them that gifts had never unlocked.

He told me later, "When I stopped chasing the image of love and started giving it away freely, I realized I'd been rich the whole time. Not in money. In capacity. I always had love to give. I just didn't know it counted until I couldn't give anything else."

Freedom from the Need to Prove

You are allowed to enjoy nice things. This is not a chapter about guilt, about renouncing pleasure, about pretending that material comforts do not matter. You can love fashion, the way fabric falls, the confidence a well-chosen outfit provides. You can love success, the satisfaction of accomplishment, the doors that achievement opens. You can love travel, luxury, the beautiful things this world offers. All of it.

But let these things be an extension of your joy, not the evidence of your worth. Let them be expressions of a life well-lived, not proof that you deserve to live. There is a difference between enjoying abundance and depending on it. Between appreciating nice things and needing them to feel okay about yourself.

Because abundance without gratitude is emptiness in disguise. You can have everything and feel nothing. You can accumulate endlessly and still be unsatisfied. The hedonic treadmill keeps moving, requiring more and more to produce the same feeling, until no amount is enough.

And humility without self-worth is just self-neglect wearing a halo. Do not confuse smallness with spirituality. Do not mistake self-deprecation for virtue. You can be humble and still know your value. You can be grounded and still stand tall.

Own your blessings unapologetically. Do not shrink from what you have accomplished or what you have been given. Do not perform poverty while enjoying abundance. But remember this: What truly makes you magnetic is not what is in your bag. It is what is in your spirit.

People are not ultimately drawn to your possessions. They are drawn to your presence. To the peace you carry. To the way you make them feel. To the spirit that animates everything else. That is what lasts. That is what matters. That is what no change in circumstance can take away.

Love as a Daily Practice

You do not have to wait for big moments to feel love. It is not reserved for weddings and births and reunions and milestones. It is available in every ordinary moment, hiding in plain sight, waiting to be noticed.

It is in the morning light on your skin. The warmth that arrives without effort, without cost, without earning. The gift that greets you simply for being here another day.

It is in laughter that makes your stomach hurt. The kind you cannot control, cannot manufacture, cannot force. The joy that erupts unexpectedly and reminds you that you are alive, that life can still surprise you, that delight is still possible.

It is in the quiet relief of forgiving yourself. The exhale after you finally release the guilt you have been carrying. The lightness that comes when you stop punishing yourself for being human.

Love is a practice, not a performance. It is not about looking loving or being perceived as loving. It is about the actual living of love, day by day, choice by choice, moment by moment.

It is found in the smallest choices. What you read: Does it fill you or drain you? How you rest: Do you actually rest, or just pause before more activity? Who you allow near your peace: do they nourish it or disturb it?

When you live with love as your oxygen, breathing it in as naturally as air, you stop suffocating from expectations. The weight lifts. The pressure eases. You no longer need to prove anything or become anything. You simply are, and that is enough.

You start breathing in gratitude. Not the forced kind that feels like another obligation, but the natural kind that arises when you actually notice what is already good. When you stop rushing past blessings on your way to more blessings. When you let what you have be enough, at least for this moment.

Spiritual Reflection

Even Jesus paused to rest. The one who came to save the world still withdrew. Still found solitude. Still took time away from the crowds and the demands and the endless need that surrounded Him. He went to quiet places to pray, to breathe, to reconnect with the Father.

He understood something we often forget: Pouring out without refilling is spiritual suffocation. You cannot give what you do not have. You cannot sustain what you do not replenish. The well must be filled for water to be drawn.

"Love your neighbor as yourself." (Mark 12:31)

That was not a suggestion. It was an equation. A mathematical relationship between two variables. The love you give to your neighbor is connected to, proportional to, and limited by the love you give to yourself. You cannot love your neighbor more than yourself and sustain it. The equation does not balance that way.

Because how you love yourself is how you teach others to love you. The standard you accept becomes the standard they understand. What you tolerate from yourself, you will tolerate from others.

What you offer yourself, you will know how to offer others.

And how you teach the world to love again. One interaction at a time. One moment of kindness at a time. One refusal to perpetuate the cycle of depletion at a time. You model what healthy love looks like, and the world learns from your example.

Hard Truths (Wrapped in Grace)

The world does not need your perfection. It needs your peace. It does not need you to have everything figured out. It needs you to be present, grounded, and available. Imperfect and still loving.

You cannot heal what you hate, not in others, not in yourself. Healing requires compassion. It requires acceptance of what is before it can become what will be. Hate only creates more of what it opposes.

Kindness does not make you naïve. It makes you necessary. The world has enough cynics, enough hardened hearts, enough people who have decided that kindness is weakness. It needs people brave enough to be kind anyway.

Being open is not a weakness. It is the highest form of strength. Anyone can build walls. Anyone can armor themselves against connection. It takes courage to remain open. To risk being hurt. To keep loving anyway.

Success without a soul is just noise. Achievement without meaning is just motion. You can accomplish everything and still feel empty if you have lost yourself in the accomplishment.

"If the heart could speak, it would say: 'I don't need you to fix the world. Just remember what it feels like to love it.'"

Journal Prompts

What simple joys have I been overlooking lately? What is already good that I have been rushing past?

How can I love beyond my comfort zone, across culture, faith, or difference? What would that require of me?

What would it look like if I made love, not fear, my daily oxygen? How would my days be different?

Where do I need to put my oxygen mask on first? What have I been neglecting in myself while trying to serve others?

Affirmation

I am love in motion. I breathe peace into my home, my work, and my world. I am not chasing perfection. I am cultivating presence. I fill myself first so I can pour into others from overflow, not depletion.

Closing Truth

You were never meant to live with an empty heart. That was not the design. That was not the intention. You were created for fullness, for overflow, for the kind of love that has enough to spare.

Love was always meant to be your oxygen. Not a luxury for special occasions. Not a reward for accomplishment. Your essential breath. Your constant companion. Your guide back to gratitude, grace, and grounded humanity.

So take a deep breath. Let it fill your lungs, your chest, your whole being. Feel the air enter and know that you are alive, that you are here, that this moment is yours.

Exhale the striving. Release the constant effort to prove, to achieve, to become acceptable. Let it go with your breath. It is not serving you. It never was.

Inhale the softness. Let gentleness enter where striving used to live. Let kindness fill the space that anxiety once occupied. Let love take up residence in the home of your heart.

Welcome back. To your heart, which has been waiting for you. To your truth, which has been speaking beneath the noise. To the sacred simplicity of being human, of loving and being loved, of giving and receiving, of breathing in and breathing out.

Because when you love better, the world breathes easier. One person at a time. One moment at a time. One breath at a time. Starting with you. Ending with everyone your life touches.

This is what it means to love better. Not perfectly. But presently. Not dramatically. But daily. Not for show. But for soul.

You are ready. You have always been ready. Now go. Be love. Breathe love. Live love.

The world is waiting.

~

As we close this journey together, let us carry these truths forward into a final reflection: the lasting impact of loving better.

EPILOGUE

Why We Love. Why We Exist.

"We are not here to perfect love.
We are here to remember that we already are it."

The Soul's Gentle Truth

There comes a moment in every woman and man's journey

when all the titles, triumphs, heartbreaks, and lessons blur into one sacred question:

"Why am I here?"

We chase answers in achievement.

We seek them in relationships, in wealth, in healing, in applause.

But eventually, all roads lead back to the same place

the heart.

Because beneath every desire is the same divine longing:

to give love,

to receive love,

to be love.

We exist to remember that.

The Purpose Beneath It All

You are not here merely to survive.

You are not here to perform worthiness or prove divinity.

You are here to embody it.

Every challenge that broke you open was not punishment, it was preparation.

Every relationship that tested you was not failure, it was formation.

Every loss, every tear, every surrender was life carving space for a greater truth:

that you were never unworthy, just unfinished.

Love isn't the goal. It's the language of your soul.

You are here to speak it in your work, your words, your presence.

Story: The Man Who Asked Why

A man once said to me,

"I've worked hard all my life, built everything I was told to,

but sometimes I wake up and wonder, what's it all for?"

I asked him, "When was the last time you laughed, really laughed?"

He said, "When my daughter hugged me and told me I'm her favorite superhero."

And there it was.

Purpose revealed not in success, but in connection.

Not in the legacy of doing, but in the legacy of being.

That's why we exist.

To love and be loved in a way that leaves the world softer because we were here.

Why the World Needs Your Light

Every time you choose peace over pride,

you heal something ancient in the human story.

Every time you forgive when you could condemn,

you shift the collective frequency closer to grace.

Every time you tell the truth kindly,

you teach others that honesty and compassion can coexist.

The world doesn't need more power.

It needs more presence.

More people who remember that being human was never a punishment; it was the Creator's favorite expression.

A Soft Return to Wonder

As children, we loved without hesitation.

We laughed easily, forgave quickly, and believed boldly.

Then life happened and we built walls to survive it.

But you are not here to die behind those walls.

You are here to take them down brick by brick,

until your soul can feel sunlight again.

To wake up in awe of small miracles, breath, laughter, sunrise, silence.

To see divinity not as something to chase, but something that already lives in you.

That is the quiet revolution of loving better:

reclaiming wonder in a world that forgot how to look up.

The Mystery of Existence

We may never fully understand the why of existence

why stars burn or hearts break,

why souls meet, why time moves.

But perhaps the point was never to understand.

Perhaps it was to experience.

To feel.

To fall and rise.

To cry and still choose joy.

To lose and still choose love.

To walk each day with reverence

knowing that to exist at all is grace.

Because every breath is proof of purpose.

And every act of love is proof of God.

Spiritual Reflection

"We love because He first loved us." - 1 John 4:19

Love is not what we do.

It's what we return to over and over, through heartbreak and healing, through loss and laughter.

You were never asked to be perfect.

You were asked to be present.

To live as evidence that love is still alive in human form.

Reader's Reflection, The Final Invitation

Take a moment.

Breathe deeply.

Place your hand over your heart.

That rhythm? That pulse? That is purpose.

You are here to love.

To create.

To forgive.

To learn.

To begin again.

You are not late.

You are not lost.

You are exactly where love needed you to be right here, remembering.

Affirmation

I am here to love not perfectly, but truthfully.

I am light, learning how to shine in human form.

I am divine breath made visible,

and every day I live with love is a day I fulfill my purpose.

Closing Benediction

May you walk gently through the world

knowing that you are both the question and the answer.

The prayer and the proof.

The seed and the bloom.

May you love better

not to be seen,

but to see.

Not to be right,

but to be real.

And when the world forgets what love looks like,

may your life remind it.

A Letter to My Future Children

"You are not here to fix the world.

You are here to love it and in doing so, you'll heal what needs mending."

My beloved children,

By the time you read this, I hope you already know that real love is not something you earn.

It's the air you breathe. The rhythm of your soul. The quiet truth you were born from.

You are not an accident.

You are an answered prayer wrapped in divine purpose.

I wrote this book before you arrived,

when the world felt noisy and many hearts were afraid to love out loud.

I wanted to leave something that would remind you

not of what to do, but of who you are.

You are love in human form.

When the World Tries to Tell You Who to Be

There will be days when the world tries to convince you that success is louder than peace, that popularity matters more than purpose,

that beauty is something you chase instead of something you are.

Don't believe it.

You were born with everything you'll ever need to be enough.

You don't have to prove your worth; you only have to remember it.

And when life gets loud, when people misunderstand your softness,

I pray you'll never trade your truth for approval.

Because the world doesn't need more people who blend in.

It needs souls brave enough to stand in their light kindly, fiercely, faithfully.

If You Ever Feel Lost

Come home.

Not to a place but to yourself.

Close your eyes.

Breathe.

Listen for the whisper that sounds like love. That's God. That's me. That's you.

The world will teach you about strength,

but I hope you'll remember that true strength is gentleness that stays kind in chaos.

That real power is peace.

To my daughter and the little girl in me

May you walk with grace that cannot be bought,

and confidence that cannot be shaken.

You don't have to dim your light to be loved.

You don't have to choose between ambition and softness.

You can be both a lion and a lullaby.

When you love, love with truth.

When you give, give with wisdom.

And when you rise, reach back and pull another woman with you.

Remember, being feminine is not a weakness.

It's a divine strategy, the quiet force that brings warmth to the world.

To My son

May you grow into men who protect without pride,

lead without control,

and love without fear.

Strength is not in how loud you roar

it's in how gently you listen.

When you meet women, honor them.

Not because they are fragile,

but because they are sacred.

Let empathy be your armor.

Let truth be your reputation.

Let kindness be your legacy.

And never be ashamed to feel.

Real men cry. Real men pray. Real men love deeply that's where their strength begins.

When You Choose Love

Love will not always be easy.

It will stretch you, test you, break you open, and make you whole again.

Sometimes, you'll walk away to protect your peace.

Other times, you'll stay and learn patience.

But always choose the kind of love that feels like truth

the one that brings you closer to yourself, not further away.

When You Doubt Your Purpose

Remember: you were not made to chase meaning.

You are meaning.

You are light wearing skin,

and every act of love, no matter how small, is a sacred offering to life itself.

Hold compassion like currency.

Trade in empathy.

Spend your joy freely there is more where it came from.

And when you succeed, remember that success means nothing if your soul feels empty.

Let your peace be your proof.

What I've Learned About Life

Life won't always go as planned.

Sometimes God will close doors because He knows the room beyond them will suffocate your spirit.

Sometimes you'll lose what you wanted most to make room for what you truly need.

When that happens, I pray you'll trust the pause.

Even silence is sacred if you're listening for direction.

Don't be afraid to begin again

even a thousand times.

My Prayer for You

May you love deeply without losing yourself.

May you walk in humility and rise in power.

May you learn to see God not only in church,

but in laughter, in music, in nature, in strangers.

May you know that joy is holy.

And may you understand that loving yourself is not vanity, it's stewardship.

Because when your heart is full, you will heal everyone you touch.

The Legacy I Leave You

This book, these words, this love

they are not instructions.

They are inheritance.

I wrote them because I wanted you to know:

You come from a lineage that chose healing over bitterness.

You come from women who refused to shrink.

You come from men who remembered how to feel.

You come from love and you were born to expand it.

Final Words

If ever you forget who you are,

look for love in the smallest things

a sunrise, a child's laugh, a stranger's kindness.

That's where God hides.

And when you remember Him, you'll remember you.

You are not alone.

You never were.

You never will be.

Love, always and in all ways,

- *Anze*

Made in the USA
Coppell, TX
24 February 2026

72232742R00142